Young Adults

Engage the Bible

push it!

Young Adults

Engage

the Bible

push it!

volume 4

United Church Press, Cleveland, Ohio 44115

www.ucpress.com

© 2003 by United Church Press

Printed in the United States of America on acid-free paper

07   06   05   04   03   02   5   4   3   2   1

ISBN 0-8298-1583-X

CONTENTS

INTRODUCTION: WHAT'S THE PUSH ALL ABOUT?

1

Welcome to this fourth volume of *Push It!* As with the three previous volumes of this Bible study for young adults, you are again invited to approach the Bible with your distinctive expectations. You are encouraged to start where you are, to "push" the scripture, and then to get "pushed" in new and challenging ways.

What expectations do you bring to the Bible? Are any of the following attitudes similar to yours?

- When I read the Bible, I'll know what to do and how to live my life. It gives guidelines for living.

- It's a bizarre book, full of all kinds of visions of the world. Some of the pictures it paints of the world—the way the world should be and how people act—are important to imagine. I want those ideas floating around in my mind and gut as I figure out what to do with my life.

- I really want to know God; it's a spiritual thing. I figure the Bible is about God. It'll help me get to God.

- The Bible has always been important to the church, to lots of people in the United States and Canada. Because it seem so important, I ought to consider looking at it now. I guess I'll check it out to see if it has some real value.

- I don't know a thing about the Bible, but I am curious. I want to look at it and see if it has anything of significance to offer.

- The ways people have used the Bible seem to have messed up a lot of things. I want to wrestle with it myself and see if it says all the things that people think it says.

Push It! recognizes these varieties of experiences and expectations that you and other young adults bring to the Bible. As it leads you into the study of the Bible, perhaps you will be surprised at the attitudes and expectations that surface for you.

Push It! makes some assumptions about the expectations of young adults, assumptions you can test. At least three assumptions led to the concept of "push it" and all the pushing that goes on in this volume.

The first assumption is the concept of "push." Push is the energy that many young adults bring to a task before them—grounded in their own experience of the world. To push is to test something's truth and its relevancy for life.

Push is similar to what Tom Beaudoin has characterized as "the irreverent spiritual quest of Generation X."[1] Both society and the church teach about religious meaning through media, technology, sciences, and tradition. Young adults, as creators and receivers of that culture, often work outside the traditional box asking questions or making connections that other adults may overlook. Cynicism, irreverence, and attitude may characterize this push.

In this study guide, we perceive such irreverence as a spiritual gift. That gift is evident in the expectations about the Bible suggested above—the demand for truth and relevancy. It is a gift, touched by God's sometimes discomforting spirit, that authentically demands a connection between the world today, the world of young adults, and the ancient tradition of the Christian faith. The push is also a prophetic gift that young adults may bring to both church and culture—exposing hypocrisy, demanding truth, and leading to acts of justice and love. Each session will invite you to push the text, explore your questions, and connect with your life.

A second assumption is that the Bible is a great source of religious imagination for young adults. Along with irreverence, imagination and idealism are often pointed to as vital characteristics of young adults. When you try to figure out what you want to do with your life, or with whom you want to be, or what is important to you, what do you do? You imagine. You paint a picture of your world as you see it, start to identify your calling and future, and go to work on it. Daniel Levinson has characterized the task of young adulthood as the formation of a "dream."[2] Such idealism may inspire and lead you—maybe powerfully reemerging throughout your life.

The images, stories, characters, and words of the Bible provide a stage on which to gain—sometimes by opposing, sometimes by accepting—God's biblical imagination. You may challenge the Bible out of your vision. The Bible, however, may paint an alternative imagination for you—pushing you. Perhaps you will see a vision of the world different from the injustice and violence in the world around you. *Push It!* is designed to help you imaginatively experience the Bible—to explore it with head and heart. It also is designed for you to play with, challenge, and act on the images that emerge out of study.[3]

The third assumption is the role of and need for engagement with others. Who inspires you? To whom do you look to help you figure things out? Who pushes you in a way that brings out the best in you? Whom do you want to be around to test your ideas, party, feel at home, or reveal your heart? Whom do you want to care for? As with many young adults, you may experience a shift in how you relate to others from your years as a teenager. Now others are as important to direct and shape your lifework in the world, as they are for love and acceptance. You may look to a mentor, teacher, work supervisor, coworker, or relative to push and be pushed by. At the same time, you may be a Big Brother or Sister, volunteer, or mentor to someone else expressing and testing your vision of the world. With peers at school, work, church, and elsewhere, you may both care for and push one another. You may take stands that sometimes are in solidarity with others, but sometimes stand against others, expressing the gifts of both irreverence and idealism.

When you approach the Bible, your personal interest may be foremost in your mind. You may also look at it with others—challenging others, listening to others, praying with others, and critically viewing how others live it in the world. This volume encourages you to work together with other young adults and to learn from one another. Together you push the Bible and listen to it.

Push It! also pushes you to move out from study alone and into the world of others—taking stands and serving others.

Push It! is also part of a larger Bible study program for all ages. As a young adult component in BIBLE QUEST: A BIBLE STORY CURRICULUM FOR ALL AGES, almost all of the thirteen Bible stories and passages included are also explored in materials available for all ages.* As part of your engagement with others, consider studying the passages with persons of other ages. Try leading a group of young children or junior high youth. Explore the passages with older adults. You may discover their challenges and insights, their own pushes, will challenge and inspire you.

Whatever expectations you bring to the Bible, whatever passions you bring to life, these are spiritual gifts that may be used for engaging the Bible. The hope is that *Push It!* will help you in an irreverent, imaginative, and communal discovery of God through the Bible.

O God, you gave me life. I am going to push you to push me to make the most of it. Amen.

Sidney D. Fowler

Minister for Worship, Liturgy, and Spiritual Formation

Local Church Ministries: A Covenanted Ministry of

The United Church of Christ, Cleveland, Ohio

*For information about BIBLE QUEST materials for other ages, contact your denominational publisher or United Church Press at 800.537.3394 or <ucpress@ucc.org>.

1.   Tom Beaudoin, *Virtual Faith: The Irreverent Spiritual Quest of Generation X* (San Francisco: Jossey-Bass Publishers, 1998).
2.   Daniel Levinson et al., *The Seasons of a Man's Life* (New York: Ballantine Books, 1979), 91–97.
3.   For more on young adults, imagination, faith, and the Bible, see Beaudoin, *Virtual Faith*, 155; Sharon Parks, *The Critical Years: The Young Adult Search for a Faith to Live By* (San Francisco: Harper & Row, 1986), 108–58; and Walter Brueggemann, *Texts under Negotiation: The Bible and Postmodern Imagination* (Minneapolis: Fortress Press, 1993).

HOW TO USE *PUSH IT!* 1

WHY USE THIS GUIDE?

Push It! is a thought-provoking guide designed to act as a springboard for your spiritual reflection. The sessions in this resource contain contemporary poems and stories, musings on current films, books, art, and music. This guide also contains some of the most dynamic stories of the Bible. You are given opportunities to ask critical questions of these ancient texts, while being challenged by the issues and concerns raised by these stories.

Individuals can use *Push It!* as the basis for personal study or meditation. Groups will also find the guide useful as a resource for a variety of educational programs, particularly those designed for young adults. The book may also be used as part of the program BIBLE QUEST: A BIBLE STORY CURRICULUM FOR ALL AGES.

Push It! was developed with the assumption that you bring your experiences, doubts, challenges, conversations, and hopes with you when you study the Bible. These concerns enrich that study, making the Bible relevant while pushing you to reassess some of your assumptions. Your questions about the world around you, as well as your critical questions about biblical stories, are a vital part of your spirituality. It is our hope that you will bring these questions to your study of the Bible while being open to having the Bible "push" you in new directions.

The writers of *Push It!* believe that the Bible tells the story of real people who struggled with some of the same personal and social challenges we face today. Concerns about relationships, war, social change, famine, money, inequality, and rural and urban life were as familiar to our biblical ancestors as they are to us. Discovering these connections between past and present, we may experience hope and fresh energy to address these challenges.

Each session in *Push It!* opens with an artifact of modern life—a poem, story, reflection, cry for justice, or emotional dilemma—that sheds light on the spiritual dimension of our lives. These expressions of human conflict, joy, and desire are set beside biblical stories that express similar emotions and challenges. Through questions and activities, you are invited to experience the dialogue between the past and present, between our struggles and those of our biblical ancestors. Feel free to contribute your questions and insights to the dialogue. Contrast your writing, art, and music with the biblical stories, and allow those stories to return the favor—enriching the creativity within you.

THE MOVEMENT OF THE SESSIONS

Each session of this guide begins with a title that indicates the focus of the session. The title is followed by a verse that seems to express at least one theme of the biblical story that will be explored. A modern comment follows the verse, connecting our lives with the lives of our biblical ancestors.

LIFE'S A PUSH

This section of the session starts with a story, poem, meditation, image, movie scene, song, or scenario that may connect with some of your experiences. This is followed by a series of questions that enable you to reflect on your life and the hopes, disappointments, and dreams you are facing. If you are using the questions for group discussion, feel free to omit or add questions. A short prayer is included to ground your exploration in all that is holy and to recall that God is with you in your spiritual quest.

THE STORY

A Bible story is provided within the body of each session. Most often these stories are reprinted from the *New Revised Standard Version*, a 1989 translation by the Division of Christian Education of the National Council of the Churches of Christ in the United States.

Read the biblical story carefully, then choose a way to experience the story from the many provided in "Ideas for Deepening the Connection to the Bible" on pages 12–26. You may want to think about the ways the focus issue is raised in "Life's a Push" as you choose your method of experiencing the story.

You Push the Story

In "You Push the Story," you are invited to explore pushes. Pushes are the challenges you may want to raise about the Bible passages. They include questions about things that seem unbelievable, wrong, confusing, or compelling in a story. These are the questions with which you may long to confront the writers of these stories or the community they were written for.

Many push possibilities are provided in this guide. We encourage you to add your own to this list. Use them as a jumping-off point for your reflections or group discussion. Keep in mind that some of your concerns may also be explored in "The Story Behind the Story" section in each session.

This guide is intended to be a user-friendly tool. Don't be afraid to make notes in the margins of the Bible story. Highlight phrases or questions that are significant to you.

The Story Pushes You

In this section, the Bible pushes back with questions that will challenge your assumptions and provide new insights and perspectives. You will be encouraged to think about the ways the Bible offers comfort or challenge, judgment or healing. Opportunities will be provided to reexamine your beliefs and actions through the lens of the characters, stories, and faith experiences expressed in the Bible.

Once again you will be offered a series of push possibilities. However, these will focus on the ways in which the Bible pushes you. Add your pushes to this list. Take time to write in a journal about the impact of these pushes on your spiritual journey.

THE STORY BEHIND THE STORY

Each biblical story was developed in a particular context, time, and place. In "The Story Behind the Story," you will learn more about the background to the biblical story. Information is provided about the times in which the Bible story was written, the community of the story's original hearers, and about the issues and concerns the story was written to address. Historical information, the meaning of words and phrases, and the ways in which early faith communities lived and functioned are examined.

PUSH OUT

Faith and biblical insight doesn't begin and end with individual reflection. It is always set in the community in which we live—both local and global. In this part of the session you are invited to express, through concrete actions, the insights you have gained. Possibilities for social action, retreats, and community service are provided. Art, film, music, and literary suggestions are included. However, these are only starting places. Add your ideas and those of others to these suggestions. If you are participating in a group study, you may find that these push-out ideas will help you expand your study beyond thirteen weeks.

If you are using this guide for individual reflection, we encourage you to think of others in your community with whom you might share some of the insights you have gained. The stories in *Push It!* are great to share over coffee with a friend, or with someone you know who is struggling with the same issues raised in this guide.

GROUP IDEAS

There is a final page in each session that outlines ways to structure group sessions.

Under "Life's a Push," you will find warm-up activities, suggestions for creating a pleasant atmosphere, and ideas for worship or centering. Group ideas for "You Push the Story" and "The Story Pushes You" include suggestions for engaging the group in push possibilities. Concrete ideas on how to lay out "The Story Behind the Story" are provided under group ideas. Ways to end sessions are suggested at the close of the "Push Out" section.

INDIVIDUAL USE

There are many ways to use this guide for individual reflection. Individual persons may want to meditate on the biblical stories and the musings on modern life. Persons can respond to the push possibilities in their journals. The poems and prayers, and discussions of music and art, can also act as a springboard to one's creativity. Individual persons may want to paint, draw, or write about the ideas raised in the sessions. They may also find information and ideas that will help them with community projects that they are involved in. Those who choose to use *Push It!* for individual study should feel free to skip around the sessions, using the sections that seem to speak to them about their specific concerns.

Whether you use this guide for individual or group study, find people to dialogue with about the concerns raised here. The insights you gain are valuable and are meant to be shared in community.

USING THE RESOURCE IN A GROUP CONTEXT

There are thirteen sessions in this book. They can be used in a variety of group settings, including Bible or study groups, church school for young adults, retreats, work camps, fellowship groups, service or outreach committees. *Push It!* is also a great resource for university or campus ministry. The ideas and stories in each session can be pulled out and used either as a reflection to open a meeting or as a starting place for an in-depth discussion of a challenging topic. *Push It!* is a flexible guide that can be adapted to different settings and to various time frames.

Groups may want to share the facilitation of each session, or designate a single facilitator. Sessions can be held weekly, biweekly, or monthly, depending on the time and commitment of the group members. Your group may also wish to focus on only a few of the sessions. They may want to address particular concerns raised by these sessions (such as grief, loss, or justice concerns). The writers of this resource recommend that you feel free to use the resource in whatever way best suits the needs and concerns of your group.

Many groups take a study-action-reflection approach. This is similar to the approach taken in this guide. Opportunities for biblical exploration are provided, along with ideas for community action. Prayer, reflections on scripture, and meditation ideas are also included. These in turn lead back to more study of scripture, and the call to act in response to the biblical witness. All of this is set in the context of community—both the biblical community of ancient times and the modern community of those struggling to live out their faith as disciples of Christ.

Those who are already working in social justice or community service groups often find that they are emotionally drained by the often daunting work that they are doing. In *Push It!* a hopeful vision of social concerns and biblical values is explored. This will be refreshing to those who commit themselves to this kind of witness. It may also offer some sense of spiritual grounding for the work they are doing.

Retreats can also be designed using the sessions provided in this guide. Retreats provide an opportunity for groups to spend more time discussing the push possibilities and developing concrete responses to the "Push Out" ideas. Several sessions are ideal for retreats. The session on the story of Abigail and David from 1 Samuel 25:2–39, 42b would make a good weekend focused on peacemaking. Groups could make a fun actors' workshop retreat out of the stories from Acts in sessions 11 and 12. Vision and mission planning retreats would be enriched by the material in the final session based on Revelation

7:9–17; grounding vision and mission for the future could come from recollecting stories of the past using the session "Stones of Memory." Other combinations or single sessions might jump out at you as good explorations for retreat settings, depending on the needs and interests of your group.

EXPANDING THE RESOURCE BEYOND THIRTEEN WEEKS

Groups may wish to use this resource for more than thirteen sessions. Sessions can be broken down into two or three shorter sessions. Or if groups want longer sessions, they can add to the sessions before they break them apart. For instance, more push possibilities can be added to sessions. Multiple options for reading and/or experiencing the story can be used.

When groups are excited about the issues raised in a particular session, you may want to add a session to continue the conversation. Speakers can be invited and/or the group can create its own session outline based on the outline provided the week before.

More sessions can be developed to focus on developing and implementing "Push Out" ideas. These sessions will require planning and group input, especially those that involve learning about community service opportunities or planning retreats. It may be that your group will develop a pattern of meeting once to experience the material in the session, once to plan push-outs, and a third time to engage in the "Push Out" activity.

When your group ends its study, mark the occasion in some way that is significant for the participants. You may want to plan and share a special worship time or celebrate with a party or shared meal. Express the sense of community you have experienced together as you have pushed your spiritual growth.

IDEAS FOR DEEPENING THE CONNECTION TO THE BIBLE

1

You will be asked in each session of *Push It!* to read and experience the focus Bible story for that session. First, read the story found in the "Story" section of the session. Then, experience the story through one or more of the methods described below.

These methods are meant to provide variety in deepening your connection with the Bible stories. They can be used by either individual readers or groups. The thoughts, feelings, and conversations sparked by the "Life's a Push" movement of the session can help you decide which method of engaging each particular story might be most meaningful or illuminating. Experiment with a variety of methods as you move through the sessions. Also, consider trying multiple methods with the same story to extend the use of the sessions in this guide.

WHY READING THE STORIES ISN'T ENOUGH

If we bring what's important to us—our struggles and dreams, our feelings and ideas—and seek to enter its many worlds, the Bible comes alive. The Bible stories in *Push It!* challenge us to come to them with our whole selves and all of our senses. We are invited to truly relate to the characters, listen in on the questions and arguments they raise, and float along the Bible's rivers of plots. That's what these experiential methods are: invitations to merge ourselves, our gifts, our personalities, and current questions into the power of the story.

The well-known professor and theologian Martin Buber wrote, "A story must be told in such a way that it constitutes help in itself. My grandfather was lame. Once they asked him to tell a story about his teacher. And he related how his teacher used to hop and dance while he prayed. My grandfather rose as he spoke, and he was so swept away by his story that he began to hop and dance to show how the master had done. From that hour he was cured of his lameness. That's how to tell a story."[1]

That's how to tell a biblical story. To bring our whole mind, body, and spirit into the Bible story and then forget ourselves in its allure so that we might be transformed.

Eugene Peterson writes, "Good storytelling involves us in what has been sitting right in front of us for years but that we hadn't noticed or hadn't thought was important or hadn't thought had anything to do with us. And then we do notice—the story wakes us up to what is there and has always been there. . . . The Scriptures, simply by virtue of their narrative form, draw us into a reality in which we find ourselves in touch with the very stuff of our humanity, what we sense in our bones counts."[2] Perceptions from stories bear seeds in our thinking through reading and discussion. For these perceptions to grow and take root in our lives, there is a tending, a germination that occurs through actions which prepare us to hear and see and reflect. Often transformation occurs in the midst of actions that plant perceptions in spaces where they find nurture. It's much more than simply setting our minds to the story. It is setting our whole way of being to the story.

Often the stories of the Bible invite us to take particular actions. The form of the message of God-with-us suggests the function of our engaging the message: active, creative, embodied, communal, meditative activity. Bible stories are stories of an active God woven together with stories of human activity. Consider Denise Levertov's poem, "The Task":

> As if God were an old man
> always upstairs, sitting about
> in sleeveless undershirt, asleep,
> arms folded, stomach rumbling,
> his breath from open mouth
> strident, presaging death . . .
> No, God's in the wilderness next door
> —that huge tundra room, no walls and a sky roof—
> busy at the loom. Among the berry bushes,
> rain or shine, that loud clacking and whirring,

irregular but continuous;
God is absorbed in work, and hears the spacious hum of bees, not
the din,
and hears far-off
our screams. Perhaps
listens for prayers in that wild solitude.
And hurries on with the weaving:
till it's done, the great garment woven,
our voices, clear under the familiar
blocked-out clamor of the task,
can't stop their
terrible beseeching. God
imagines it sifting through, at last, to music
in the astounded quietness, the loom idle,
the weaver at rest.[3]

CHOOSING A METHOD

The method you choose for a story is influenced by a number of factors: the form of the Bible story, the realities that have bubbled up in "Life's a Push," the diversity of ways that we as humans come to know and engage the world, and the comfort level of the group experiencing the sessions.

If the Bible passage is a narrative with characters and plot, methods of acting out the story, such as readers' theater or guided meditation, can be helpful. If the passage is a visionary story like Revelation 7:9–17 you may choose methods that stretch the imagination, such as art or poetry. Some stories function inside the context of bigger stories and may require methods that allow for those bigger stories to be known, like the extra reading suggested for sessions on Jonah and David.

Thoughts and feelings raised in "Life's a Push" can direct choice as well. Difficult, more personal themes require sensitive levels of engagement that allow participants greater degrees of safety in what they share. Joyful, expansive imagery in scenarios may suggest movement and creativity. Methods which begin with individual work will be more appropriate to themes that invite introspection, while themes focused on community-building may lend themselves more to group exercises.

There will be some methods with which you will feel more at home. In a group, each person will experience different comfort levels with different methods. It helps to vary the methods. Those methods with which we are initially least comfortable can, with patience and encouragement, be those that lead us to the greatest discoveries of the story and of ourselves. Building a sense of trust in oneself, in the group, and in the group facilitator will reap rewards as you begin to risk trying more adventuresome ways of experiencing the stories.

Differences in individual comfort levels with particular methods of experiencing Bible stories may be due to the fact that we each encounter the world with a unique mix of intelligences. Howard Gardner in his book *Frames of Mind* identifies at least eight different intelligences by which persons learn and interact with the world. They are:

Logical-Mathematical Intelligence–the ability to learn through abstract symbols, the testing of hypotheses, and the search for patterns among ideas or objects. Working logical puzzles, outlining, and sequencing engage this intelligence.

Naturalistic Intelligence–the ability to observe nature, define it, and care for it. Growing things, observing nature, and working with animals are examples of this.

Bodily Kinesthetic Intelligence–the ability to use tactile senses and the body to understand things. Miming, dancing, and playing active games are examples.

Visual-Spatial Intelligence–the ability to see and create images such as drawings, maps, and sculptures.

Verbal-Linguistic Intelligence–the ability to use words in writing, speaking, reading, and listening. Storytelling, debating, and working crossword puzzles engage this intelligence.

Musical Intelligence–the ability to use sound, rhythm, and tone through listening to songs, tapping, and playing musical instruments.

Interpersonal Intelligence–the ability to form relationships with others. Playing group games, leading discussions, and participating in cooperative projects engage this intelligence.

Intrapersonal Intelligence–focuses on the interior of our lives. Things like journaling, silent reflection, guided meditation, or daydreaming express and support this gift.

Underlying Gardner's description of the phenomenon of multiple intelligences is that people learn in many ways and no one way of learning is better than any other. We have primary intelligences which we feel comfortable using while working to also feel comfortable engaging some of the others.[4]

As we select methods for experiencing Bible stories, it is important to be attentive to the primary intelligences engaged by the methods and to strive to create a good balance of those intelligences as we move through the sessions. The goal is to allow everyone to have an opportunity to engage those intelligences that come most naturally, as well as those that are most challenging.

LIST OF METHODS

Here are some suggested methods from which to choose:

1. USE ART.

Talk about the dominant image or images in the story and then invite artistic expression of the image or images, using tempera paint and brushes, linoleum block printing, crayons, or markers. Art is especially effective for stories that may be very familiar—Adam and Eve, Daniel in the lions' den, Jesus at the Garden of Gethsemane. Art helps us attend to the story in new ways.

For a quick activity with paint, have participants focus for five to ten minutes on the feelings that a story evokes and then paint with attention to color and texture rather than detail.

Use clay to express feelings or images that emerge from reading the story. Try shutting your eyes as you work, letting your hands do the creating and only glancing at what you are doing periodically. Clay can also be used to create characters in the story, capturing the identity-shaping action or gesture of that character.

With just about any medium, you can depict one of the scenes of a story or create a personal reaction to the story. If you are the facilitator, be clear about the focus of the art assignment so people feel comfortable starting out. Allow fifteen to twenty minutes for the work. You may want to put on quiet music. Emphasize that being artistic is not the intent of the activity, but simply being as authentic as possible. Allow time to share results as a group when people have finished. Invite the group to offer an opportunity for members to explain their creations without comment from others.

2. EXAMINE THE STORY'S STRUCTURE.

Make sure each participant has a copy of *Push It!* Have colored pencils or highlighter pens ready. In a group, people can work in pairs or as individuals.

First, underline words that are either the same or similar with the same color to see if there is any pattern to their use and placement in the story. Look also for phrases that are the same or similar and underline or highlight them. Sometimes passages are structured with repetition around central themes of the story.

If it is poetry, is there any set meter to each phrase? Read the passage aloud to see where the short and long syllables land in each line. What words or syllables are emphasized?

If it is a story, what are the different scenes? Where does the tension develop and where is the tension resolved if it is resolved? Who is the protagonist in the story?

Circle words that you want to know more about. Using a concordance— a resource book that lists all the words used in the Bible and where they can be found—available in a library's biblical studies section, look up the other instances in which your circled words appear. Pay special attention to multiple occurrences in the same book of the Bible or similar books. What does the use of these words in other passages suggest about their meaning and importance? You may also look up the words in a Bible dictionary.

Finally, if the story comes from Matthew, Mark, or Luke, see if it can be found in one or both of the other Gospels. If so, it's known as a "Gospel parallel." These stories are collected and shown side-by-side in *Gospel Parallels* (Nashville, Tenn.: Thomas Nelson, 1952), edited by Burton Throckmorton. Compare versions of the same story in different Gospels. Sometimes a story is longer or shorter than it is in another Gospel, with details changed. What is added or left out or presented differently? These distinctions may be hints to the special point the Gospel writer may be making.

3. Read the Passage in a Variety of Ways.

Try reading the story by going around a circle with each person reading a verse. Or direct several voices to read the story through in its entirety, leaving a time of silence between each reading. Or designate different voices for the characters and one voice as narrator in the form of readers' theater. Or suggest that the men read one verse and then the women read the next verse and so on, or one side of the room and then the other side, like a choral reading. Try reading the story with different kinds of music in the background or in different settings, such as outside, in a room with an echo, in a confined space, or in the dark with participants sitting around a candle. Try shouting out the passage and then reading it in a whisper. Direct one voice to read and then the rest of the group to repeat each phrase, mimicking the inflection of the solo reader. If you know someone who is familiar with American Sign Language, invite her or him to sign the passage while someone else reads it aloud. This may be especially effective with the passage from Revelation, which is so full of imagery. Try reading the story by replacing the pronoun "he" for "she" and the word "father" for "mother" when referring to God. Discuss what is revealed by the different ways of reading.

4. ACT OUT THE STORY.

Acting out the story could take the form of mime, role play, or skits. Stories in this volume that are especially suited for acting out include Zaccheus (Luke 19:1–10), Abigail (1 Samuel 2:25–39, 42b), and Paul and Silas and Lydia (Acts 16:13–40). Through mime, participants can personally experience each of the characters in the story. Spread the group out across a large open space for this activity, but have participants stay close enough so that everyone can hear the facilitator. As the facilitator introduces each of the characters, participants mime that character's actions as she or he imagines them. Give participants a chance to talk about how they felt in each role. What was it like to mime the characters? Why did they choose the gestures they used?

Role play is like mime, but people take on the speaking parts of characters as well as their actions. Sometimes role play helps capture the moods of particular portions of stories. Be sure to discuss these experiences. Have people share how playing the various roles made them feel; what insights the experience brought them; and what new appreciation of the stories they may have gained from it.

Creating skits is especially effective if you are spending more time with a passage, such as in a retreat setting where groups can take time to prepare. Different groups could prepare the same story with a different treatment. One group could prepare a pantomime, another a drama, another a musical, yet another a comedy. Groups could change the setting of the story. For instance the story of Jonah could be adapted to a contemporary setting.

Emphasize that the purpose of the activity is not to create an award-winning production but to explore the motivations, feelings, and actions of the characters—and to elicit responses to the story from the group.

If participants are not ready for these kinds of activities, invite them to sit with their eyes closed and imagine being each of the characters as excerpts are read from a story. Invite people to keep their eyes closed as they respond to discovery questions like, "In a word or phrase, how do you feel as Mary in the temple when Anna begins telling everyone about Jesus?" Or, "How would you feel as Saul, blinded by the light of God?" Or encourage participants to make entries in a journal or notebook after an imagining experience.

5. WORK WITH WORDS.

Photocopy the story and cut it up into words or phrases. See if you or the group can rebuild the story by piecing the words and phrases back together in the right order. If you can do that, then try playing with the story a bit. Move phrases around—what happens to the meaning of the story? You can also pull out key words and write them on a piece of paper or newsprint, one word per piece of paper. Together, brainstorm related words, images, phrases, or synonyms for the key words, recording them on the same sheet of paper. What fresh insights into the story emerge as you explore the words more fully?

6. WRITE YOUR OWN WORDS.

Paraphrase the story in everyday, contemporary language. If you're part of a group, have everyone share their paraphrases. Or write a parable, poem, prayer, or litany, based on the story. Make it an individual project, a project done with partners, or a group project. Writing works especially well following an experience with one of the other methods of engaging the story because people have more to draw on.

How would you paraphrase the conversation between Jesus and Nicodemus in John 3:1–17? Or the story of Eve?

7. PAIR WITH A PAINTING OR POEM.

Choose a painting, photograph, lithograph, poem, or hymn that shares a dominant image with the story and talk about how each amplifies the meaning of the other. What feelings are expressed through both or in one but not the other?

Find paintings of Jesus in the Garden at Gethsemane. How do they portray the emotions of that fateful night (Mark 14:32–50)?

8. PRAY OR MEDITATE.

Read the story slowly either silently or aloud. Do you notice any word or phrase in particular? Meditate on that word or phrase. Allow it to touch your life. What feelings, thoughts, memories, or images arise in you when you sit with it? Read the story again, reflecting on the invitation to action this word or phrase extends to you. Commit the phrase to memory.

In the quiet space of prayer, let your imagination vividly carry you to the places and scenes of the story. When you return to the group, discuss your discoveries and feelings.

9. MOVE.

If you are physically able to walk or move, spend several minutes walking or moving as if you were Saul on the road to Damascus. How do you move differently after Saul's conversion?

Move as if you are carrying the big stones out of the river Jordan in Joshua 3:7–8; 3:14–4:8. Or like one of the high priests carrying the ark of the covenant.

Watch for invitations to movement in the other sessions. Groups should be mindful of different levels of mobility when engaging stories through movement.

10. DIALOGUE WITH A CHARACTER.

Choose a character in the story with whom you would love to have a conversation. Record your "conversation" on paper. Ask the character to tell you about herself or himself. Attempt not to control the character's voice, but let it speak freely as you imagine the character. Try to relate to the character, whether or not you identify with him or her. For instance, imagine talking to Lydia or Abigail or Jonah or Zaccheus. What would you ask? How might he or she respond? What's interesting is that in writing down this "conversation" you are creating a dialogue with an inner aspect of yourself that is the character you interview. What questions and "ahas" does that bring into your faith journey?

1. Quoted in Parker Palmer, *The Active Life* (San Francisco: Jossey-Bass Publishers, 1990), 36.
2. Eugene Peterson, *Eat This Book: The Holy Communion at Table with the Holy Scripture*, Theology Today 56 (April 1999), 13–14.
3. Denise Levertov, "The Task," *Oblique Prayers: New Poems with Fourteen Translations from Jean Joubert* (New York: New Directions, 1984), 78.
4. Howard Gardner, *Frames of Mind: The Theory of Multiple Intelligences* (New York: Basic Books, 1983), 33–35.

BIBLE EXPERIENCES FOR YOUNG ADULTS

EXPERIENCE METHOD	DESCRIPTION	KIND OF BIBLE STORY
Use Art	Use paint, linoleum block print, markers, or clay. Illustrate the feeling raised or dominant image or characters of the story.	Visionary stories, words of prophecy, stories with vivid imagery.
Look at Story Structure	Use colored pens, examine words, repetition of phrases, plot line, rhythm, and shared words with other stories.	All stories; particularly helpful with poetry.
Read in Variety of Ways	Read the story using different voices, settings, musical background, inflection, and volume.	Especially effective for longer stories to get accustomed to detail. Also good for very familiar passages.
Act Out the Story	Act out characters through mime or role playing or skits focused on the motivations of characters and the feelings raised in roles.	Narrative passages. Skits best used in narratives with dialogue.
Work with Words	Cut up copy of story and move around phrases; work with synonyms for story's key words.	All stories, but especially treatise passages, letters, arguments.
Write	Paraphrase story in your own words. Write prayer, parable, song, or litany.	Good for narratives. Match kind of writing to kind of story.
Match with Painting or Poem	Look at and read story paired with painting, photo, lithograph, or poem that shares dominant image, theme, or mood with story.	Visionary passage or narrative with dominant image.
Pray for Guided Meditation	Reflect silently on words, phrases, images, or story; read and meditate on the story. Stay with word or phrase and let it conjure up thoughts, feelings, invitation.	Narratives or visionary passages.
Engage in Actions or Movement	Look at action words in story and do them.	Stories that are dominated by particular gestures or movement.
Dialogue with Character	Imagine conversation with story's character. Imagine asking questions. Write down imagined responses.	Narratives with strong characters.

ON STAYING OPEN TO THE SPIRIT

AN ARTICLE FOR *PUSH IT!*
GROUP LEADERS ON CREATING A QUALITY
LEARNING COMMUNITY
by Gloria Otis

Have you ever experienced the freedom to share, knowing that you wouldn't be judged? Have you experienced talking with someone who makes it easy for you to open up? Have you experienced a group where everyone makes you feel that it's okay to just be yourself?

I remember a group I was attending regularly where the environment was warm and inviting. I was greeted with a smile and introductions all around. I sensed an atmosphere of understanding and common ground. As the group got rolling, I felt people could identify with where I was coming from, or they were at least open to what I had to say. In short, I felt perfectly comfortable sharing.

These days, I have the opportunity to lead a bereavement support group for my church. Based on my experiences with groups that are open and inviting, I make it a priority to create an encouraging environment. As you know, if you have experienced a significant loss in your life, grief can be difficult for many people to talk about. This makes it more challenging and more important to set a tone of openness, respect, and confidentiality for the group. Leading the group requires a measure of intentionality on my part to ensure that people are as comfortable as they can be.

There are a couple of things that I practice as a part of encouraging individuals to open up in a group setting. First I try to "condition the atmosphere" with an attitude of acceptance. Acceptance has to be in the air, like the light or the fragrance of the space. Whether I agree or not with what people share, every person has to feel that his or her contribution is important. It starts with putting myself in that frame of mind. I like to think of the verse from Paul's letter to the Corinthians, "Love is patient, love is kind." (1 Corinthians 13:4). I am called to love with patience and kindness, two essential ingredients of acceptance.

Putting myself in the right frame of mind is one thing, but I can't carry the whole group atmosphere alone. The group has to agree to be open and accepting with each other. It helps to create group guidelines for conversation. Ask group members to make a list of ways they would like to treat each other and be treated. You might start with, "Take issue with the issue, not the person," or, "Don't interrupt." Ask them to describe the guidelines that would make this the safest, most engaging group they've ever experienced. Being this intentional about group process is not something we're necessarily used to and may even seem too obvious to put on paper (of course everybody knows we're not supposed to interrupt). But it can help the group and you as the leader if there are shared norms—it tells newcomers that this is a group that cares about each person, and it means you don't have to be in the lonely position of calling people to task if they transgress. When somebody repeatedly interrupts others, the whole group can take responsibility for restoring the community.

Listening to each other is perhaps the most important thing we can do in community. As the group leader, I try to model intentional listening. I've been helped in learning how to listen recently from an experience as an understudy for a play. During rehearsal the director requires that we understudies ask cast members three questions about their character. Then we have to introduce the cast members we interviewed to the rest of the company. The more we know about the characters, the more prepared we'll be if we have to take someone's place. The interviews help us make the characters come alive and help us build relationships with them. Listening well is a way to bring people alive, to validate their existence, and to build relationships with them.

Of course things like being prepared and having everything ready when people arrive helps you focus on the group members and enjoying the process. Things may not always go as you plan, and flexibility is crucial, but you having a sense of the content and basic steps of the session will give everyone confidence to participate.

The final thing to keep in mind is that your role as leader is more facilitator than professor. You don't need to be an expert in the subject matter; what you need to be good at is helping people share and feel part of the group. If no one in the group knows the answer to an important question, your role is not so much to provide an answer as it is to help the group figure out how it will make the necessary discovery.

Remember that love is patient and kind. Be patient and kind with yourself as you offer leadership. Rest in the assurance that Jesus said, "For where two or three are gathered in my name, I am there among them" (Matthew 18:20). Be open to Christ's spirit within your community and together you and the group will be able to "push it" to exciting and wondrous places of growth and faith.

Gloria Otis
Administrative Staff
Worship and Education Team
Local Church Ministries
A Covenanted Ministry of the United Church of Christ
Cleveland, Ohio; and
Director of Affinity Small Groups
Affinity Missionary Baptist Church
Cleveland, Ohio

1. [RITES OF PASSAGE

So when the woman saw that the tree was good for food, and
that it was a delight to the eyes, and that the tree was to be
desired to make one wise, she took of its fruit and ate.

Genesis 3:6a

Would you have tasted the fruit? What was Eve's
true desire?

LIFE'S A PUSH

GETTING TO THE CORE

There have been times in my life when I yearned for more—more than what I
felt my teachers could give me or even what I could find in the stories at the
libraries. As a child I was enthralled by the salty sailors in my childhood books
who left home in search of a new world. I found myself on ships, leaning over
the bow, gazing deeply into the frothy wake, partly yearning to jump in. I have
spent hours in the woods walking, craning my neck to catch sight of unfamiliar
birds or examining the veins of leaves. I have waited at the water's edge to see
dolphins breach, while dreaming of underwater life. I have walked away from
solid relationships, moved across the country, and even left the country in search
of not just a better life, but also something different. Perhaps I have been looking for myself, not sure that I could truly know myself amongst familiar faces and
streets whose names are engraved in my memory. I have also at times longed for
that which I left behind.

At my best and at my worst I am guilty of living passionately on edges of
becoming, of trying to get to the root of the matter, no matter the cost. Some
people bungee-jump, cave-dive, or parachute for thrills. Others of us refuse to
settle for easy answers or settle even for ourselves the way we are. The costs are
often high. What I hold as truth is in constant flux. There are no absolutes, and
God holds the cards. Sometimes I wish I could be simple and be satisfied with
surfaces, but I want life to "bite" me, and I want to "bite" it back. I seek wholeness through essence: a process of breaking down myself and life to base components and "whys."

I find my yearnings echoed in Fredrico Garcia Lorca's poem, "Gacela of the Dark Death."[1] At first reading, the speaker seems to wish for death but perhaps only for the death of a life that is stagnant and void of hope. The speaker says, "I want to sleep," and means, "I want to wake up." Inside the voice of the poem is possibility, a golden core. For so many of us, being young adults is like that. Struggling to know ourselves better, we reach for independence and our own greater possibilities. We continue to become ourselves—our own wholes as part of the larger whole.

GACELA OF THE DARK DEATH

I want to sleep the dream of the apples,
to withdraw from the tumult of cemeteries,
I want to sleep the dream of that child
who wanted to cut his heart on the high seas.

I don't want to hear again that the dead do not lose their blood,
that the putrid mouth goes on asking for water.
I don't want to learn of the tortures of the grass,
nor of the moon with a serpent's mouth
that labors before dawn.

I want to sleep awhile,
awhile, a minute, a century;
but all must know that I have not died;
that there is a stable of gold in my lips;
that I am the small friend of the West wind;
that I am the immense shadow of my tears.

Cover me at dawn with a veil,
because dawn will throw fistfuls of ants at me,
and wet with hard water my shoes
so that the pincers of the scorpion slide.

For I want to sleep the dream of the apples,
to learn a lament that will cleanse me of the earth;
for I want to live with that dark child
who wanted to cut his heart on the high seas.[1]

- What are some risks you have taken in the search for meaning and purpose in life? What were you hoping to gain out of the experience? What were the consequences? What were the benefits? What did you learn about yourself?

- When you learn something new and different, what happens to your old self? Do you carry the former knowledge with you? Does it die or does something else happen?

- Think of a time or conversation when something you held as a truth was challenged. How did it make you feel? Did you change your mind? How did you grow from the experience?

PRAYER

God, who created us and remains with us on our journey even when we feel most alone, we come to you in search of truth. Help us learn from our mistakes, from the risks we take, and from the questions we ask. Grant us the passion to live life to its fullest, journeying towards you in bumbling grace. Be our friend along the way. Amen.

THE STORY

Read Genesis 3:1–7 aloud, experiencing each word as you speak it. Read it as if you might be hearing a story about yourself. Try experiencing it through one of the Bible Experience ideas on page 23. What art project might help you delve more deeply into its core?

> ¹Now the serpent was more crafty than any other wild animal that the Lord God had made. He said to the woman, "Did God say, 'You shall not eat from any tree in the garden'?" ²The woman said to the serpent, "We may eat of the fruit of the trees in the garden, ³but God said, 'You shall not eat of the fruit of the tree that is in the middle of the garden, nor shall you touch it, or you shall die.' ⁴But the serpent said to the woman, "You will not die; ⁵for God knows that when you eat of it your eyes will be opened, and you will be like God, knowing good and evil. ⁶So when the woman saw that the tree was good for food, and that it was a delight to the eyes, and that the tree was to be desired to make one wise, she took of its fruit and ate; and she also gave some to her husband, who was with her, and he ate. ⁷Then the eyes of both were opened, and they knew that they were naked and they sewed fig leaves together and made loincloths for themselves.

YOU PUSH THE STORY

You have probably heard this story in one form or another many times, or at least you are familiar with it because it is part of Western culture. What did you notice this time that you haven't before? With which character do you identify most?

PUSH POSSIBILITIES FOR GENESIS 3:1–7

- Did God intend for Eve to take the fruit? Why was the tree in the garden in the first place, and why did God set it aside? Does God tempt us?

- Why did Eve take the fruit even though she knew she would be punished? What other options were available to her? Could she have found knowledge or wisdom and obeyed God at the same time?

- Why did Adam keep quiet? Was Adam just waiting for Eve to take the fruit so he did not have to take responsibility?

- Is part of human nature the desire to do that which is forbidden? Did God create that desire? Or is there another human desire at work in this story?

- What is wrong with being naked in the context of this story?

THE STORY PUSHES YOU

Let this familiar story unsettle you with its questions and possibilities. Open yourself to a new understanding. Who are you in the story?

PUSH POSSIBILITIES FOR GENESIS 3:1–7

- How does Eve's story encourage or discourage you from taking known risks in the search for knowledge and wisdom?

- In the moments when Eve reaches for the fruit, what were her thoughts? What would you have thought had you been Eve? What would you have done if you were Adam?

- What does the story teach us about ourselves, desire, and human nature?

- Do we choose to be separated from God, or does God choose to be separated from us? How separate is God? How do we bring ourselves closer to God?

- When is it okay to break rules? When is it not?

- Are there some things we shouldn't know? For example, should we know how to clone human beings?

- What relevance does this story have to our "age of information"?

THE STORY BEHIND THE STORY

The "Story of Temptation," as this passage is often called, is more ancient than perhaps even this telling. It is archetypal—designed to communicate something of the essence of the nature of humanity and God. The story assumes that there are some things that only God can know or should know. It suggests that there is a human desire to become like God. The knowledge God has, the story postulates, is available to human beings but only through disobedience. The taking of the fruit is often told as a story of sin, although there is no mention of sin.

The Hebrew language opens up a nuance in the story that is missed in English translations. The serpent is described as "craftier" (*arum*) than all the other animals God had made. The word for "naked" in Hebrew is *arummim*. Is there a link being suggested between the humans discovering that they were naked and their discovery of their own powers to be crafty? Is the shame about physical nudity or about this willingness and ability to go around God?

Another language nuance that can be lost in English is that Adam is not exempt from the encounter. In the Hebrew, the serpent's question is addressed to the singular "you." Adam passively observes the exchange between Eve and the serpent, saying nothing even though he alone had received the directive from God concerning the tree. Because archetypal stories like these are often used as prescriptions about human nature rather than descriptions, missing Adam's involvement has often led to vilifying Eve and, through her archetypal figure, all women.

For both men and women, the story is instructive about the illegitimate acquisition of wisdom. Wisdom is a process, achieved only through experience over time.

PUSH OUT

- Try to remember your childhood dreams. What did you want to be when you grew up? Are you still striving for those dreams? What keeps you going toward them, or what made you forget them? Write down those dreams and make a big poster of them you can keep on your wall to remind you what you wanted to do when the world seemed limitless. Share your dreams and posters with others who may help you reinvest in them.

- Take a long walk away from everyone and everything familiar, or take a walk in a familiar place and try to experience it anew. Ask yourself a question such as, "Why have I chosen the path in life that I am on now?" and meditate on it as you walk. Try to do it in silence, and then share your thoughts with a friend who may have done the same activity, or record your thoughts in a journal.

- Break one "rule" every day for a week. That is, do something against the grain. Spend Valentine's Day volunteering at a homeless shelter. Take part in a worship service in a different religion. Start a conversation with a person with whom you would normally avoid eye contact. Next time it rains, close your umbrella and run down the street singing, "Row, Row, Row Your Boat." Whatever—just step outside the norm and see what you learn about yourself and your world. Keep a journal.

- Check out from the library the children's book *Does God Have a Big Toe?: Stories about Stories in the Bible* (New York: Harper & Row, 1989) by Marc Gellman. What new insights do these fresh takes on old tales bring you?

GROUP IDEAS   [Focus: To experience life as a process of growth towards wisdom.

LIFE'S A PUSH

- Try to find a place outdoors or a space with a lot of natural light. Perhaps place fruits in the center of the gathering space.

- Ask one or two people to read "Gacela of the Dark Death" on page 28. Have them read it aloud twice. Make sure there are enough copies for each person to read along if they wish.

- Go through at least one of the sets of questions on pages 28–29 as a group.

- Pray together the prayer provided on page 29 or one you prefer.

THE STORY

- Have two different people read the story on page 29 aloud, one right after the other. Try to have one female and one male reading.

- Allow each person to read "The Story Behind the Story" on page 31 on their own, and then discuss it as a group.

- Have another reader read the story aloud one more time. Choose one of the Bible Experience ideas on page 23.

YOU PUSH THE STORY

- Consider the push possibilities on page 30 for Genesis 3:1–7.

- Allow the group to add their own "pushes."

THE STORY PUSHES YOU

- Explore the Push Possibilities on page 30 as a group. In addition to discussion, invite participants to write poetry or journal in response to the questions.

PUSH OUT

- Make available to the group poster paper, scraps of colored paper, old magazines, markers, and glue to make posters of their childhood dreams, and then let them share them with the group.

- Take the group on a walk in silence together, similar to traditional labyrinth walks, asking them to be intentional about choosing the question they will think about as they walk. Afterwards, invite those who are willing to share their experiences. Close with silent prayer.

2. [STONES OF MEMORY

When your children ask their parents in time to come, "What do these stones mean?" then you shall let your children know, "Israel crossed over the Jordan here on dry ground."

Joshua 4:21b–22

What parts of your story are most important? How did you commemorate them? How do you hold onto those memories?

IFE'S A PUSH

THE MEANING OF STONES

Monuments. Boulders. Pebbles. Stones collected from distant shores and hills and valleys—how do stones hold memory for us? I collect stones. I carry them in my pockets to feel the security of them. I strew them on windowsills and store them in wooden cigar boxes. They are often from beaches where I sit, praying to God to help me get through another small crisis. I have some stones from places where personal revelations came when I saw God in the drops of the waterfall. And I have stones from far-flung lands that I know I may never walk again. All are places of beauty. All are places and times I want to remember.

My family has an odd history. My sister and I were both adopted at birth into a Japanese American family. Culturally we are Japanese American. Ethnically I am Chinese American, and my sister is Korean. We hail from different lineages, different tribes. We are a mish-mash of people thrown together and challenged to love each other. Sometimes we succeed, and sometimes we do not.

Stones are scattered throughout the images I hold of my family—gravestones, river stones, and stones my mother collected from the beaches of Maine. There are hearthstones, whetstones, and cobblestone roads. And there are the collective memories of stones somewhere deep in my history: stones I have never seen that belong to my other tribe, those of my lineage, like my biological family, as well as to the greater family of living beings. Though I have never laid eyes upon these other stones, they exist nonetheless to commemorate the passages of time and stories. Somewhere, someone with parts of my genes is collecting stones. Sometime long ago, a distant relative carved large monoliths to mark astronomical movements. We are all one tribe: you, me, my family known and unknown, all those we know, and those we have yet to meet. We are closely connected some way or another by some thin thread of knowledge or DNA. Both the Bible and science say that we all go back to the same people, though they describe those first ancestors in different terms. We are each other's stories.

- What are the "stones" in your life? What are the things that bring your memories rolling back? The scent of an orange? The smell of hay? A diploma? The exhaust from a bus? A certain song and a traffic jam? An old dress? Here are some of my memories.

HOLDING ON

When I was a baby, my father would carry me out into the waves,
holding me to his chest as the water foamed around his waist.
"Farther," I would urge him, looking out to the horizon, squealing
every time a wave would catch my toes. My father went farther than I
ever expected, holding me on his shoulder as the water reached his chest,
but he never stumbled, and we never drowned.

I have cloudy memories of his father, my Oji-chan, from our stay
in Japan when I was one and a half. Oji-chan sat in the small garden,
slate slabs in a sea of river stones leading to him. Kneeling to lift me onto
his knee, he would plop his red Exxon hat on my head and offer
to take me out to the persimmon groves. We walked slowly, hand-in-
hand, through the outer gate to where the low trees grew, sunshine warm-
ing our heads. Orange, round globes filled my hands, still opaque and yet
unripe. One in each pocket, Oji-chan waved to me that it was time to go
back to lay them on the wood table, leaving enough space between so he
could sprinkle sake on them as they ripened. I came in the mornings, feeling each persimmon in the rows, finding the perfect one to offer
Oba-chan as she prepared breakfast. Now her days are filled with ochers
and violets staining thick watercolor papers. The truths I found later were
hard. Oji-chan drank himself to the family gravesite in Hiroshima before I
was age twelve. My father answered the phone at one A.M., packed his
tuxedo, hardened his face, and returned as the oldest son to bury his
father. No real surprise, quelling most emotions, he returned with formal
pictures of men in seated rows, colder than I had expected, staring at the
camera from starched positions. The burial mound sat beneath a stone
monument that was stained black from the atom bomb. Strange resting-
place.

Stories are woven now, told to me with caged joy, of Oji-chan's wrinkled face, the Exxon hat he never let anyone touch but me. I am still reeling from the care fathers show with simple gestures, not supermen heaving boulders, but our heroes, however distant and forgiven or unforgiven, loved, and crowned.

- What do your stones commemorate? Think of an important time in your life that you want to remember. Why is it important to you? What did you do to mark the occasion? Have you created something tangible to help you remember it? Do you plan to pass this memory on to others? How?

- Who are your tribes? What are the pieces of your heritage you are proud of? Ashamed of? How do you hold onto the good and reconcile the bad?

PRAYER

God, grant us strength. Help us to learn and remember the stories from all we meet. Grant us wisdom. Help us to reconcile the memories that are painful and to learn all that we can from them as we do so. Grant us peace. Amen.

THE STORY

Read the story of Joshua and the crossing of the ark of the covenant over the Jordan. Imagine the walls of water building and the feet of the priests planted in the dry bed. Feel the wonder. Remember it as a part of your family's story. Push through it with one of the options suggested on page 39.

3:7The Lord said to Joshua, "This day I will begin to exalt you in the sight of all Israel, so that they may know that I will be with you as I was with Moses. 8You are the one who shall command the priests who bear the ark of the covenant, 'When you come to the edge of the waters of the Jordan, you shall stand still in the Jordan.'"

14 When the people set out from their tents to cross over the Jordan, the priests bearing the ark of the covenant were in front of the people. 15 Now the Jordan overflows all its banks throughout the time of harvest. So when those who bore the ark had come to the Jordan, and the feet of the priests bearing the ark were dipped in the edge of the water, 16the waters flowing from above stood still rising up in a single heap far off at

Adam, the city that is beside Zarethan, while those flowing toward the sea of the Arabah, the Dead Sea, were wholly cut off. Then the people crossed over opposite Jericho. [17]While all Israel were crossing over on dry ground, the priests who bore the ark of the covenant of the Lord stood on dry ground in the middle of the Jordan, until the entire nation finished crossing over the Jordan.

[4:1] When the entire nation had finished crossing over the Jordan, the Lord said to Joshua: [2]"Select twelve men from the people, one from each tribe, [3]and command them, 'Take twelve stones from here out of the middle of the Jordan, from the place where the priests' feet stood, carry them over with you, and lay them down in the place where you camp tonight.'" [4]Then Joshua summoned the twelve men from the Israelites, whom he had appointed, one from each tribe. [5]Joshua said to them, "Pass on before the ark of the Lord your God into the middle of the Jordan, and each of you take up a stone on his shoulder, one for each of the tribes of the Israelites, [6]so that this may be a sign among you. When your children ask in time to come, 'What do those stones mean to you?' [7]then you shall tell them that the waters of the Jordan were cut off in front of the ark of the covenant of the Lord. When it crossed over the Jordan, the waters of the Jordan were cut off. So these stones shall be to the Israelites as a memorial forever."

[8]The Israelites did as Joshua commanded. They took up twelve stones out of the middle of the Jordan, according to the number of the tribes of the Israelites, as the Lord told Joshua, carried them over with them to the place where they camped, and laid them down there.

YOU PUSH THE STORY

A teacher once taught me that "myth" is a seemingly unbelievable story that embodies truth. Is this story a myth? What about this story is unbelievable? What is believable? What are its underlying truths?

PUSH POSSIBILITIES FOR JOSHUA 3:7–8; 3:14—4:8

- Why are the people crossing the Jordan?

- What is the ark of the covenant, and why would the waters of the Jordan stop because those priests were carrying it through them?

- Why was Joshua "exalted" above all others?

- Why did a representative of each tribe have to take a stone? Why were only men picked to represent the twelve tribes?

- How would generations to come tell the story of these stones?

- The better-known story of the water being stopped is of Moses and the parting of the Red Sea. Why do you think Joshua has a similar story?

THE STORY PUSHES YOU

Suspend any disbelief you hold about waters that stop to let priests walk through them. Dare to believe that the waters stopped because of the sacredness of the ark. Imagine that this is a story of your people, part of your history. What are you proud of? What do you question? What is its heritage for you? Explore these push possibilities.

PUSH POSSIBILITIES FOR JOSHUA 3:7–8; 3:14—4:8

- How does this story invite us to value a sense of heritage? How familiar are we with our heritage, our families, our faith communities, and our nations?

- History is always told from particular vantage points. What can we do to ensure we hear multiple points of view on our heritage?

- There are monuments in many countries commemorating the great victories of conquest and colonization. What do we do with these monuments? How do we interpret the milestones they represent?

THE STORY BEHIND THE STORY

Joshua is the first of the historical books of the Bible. It chronicles events after the Exodus and seeks to interpret the works of God among the people. In the opening chapter we find God commissioning Joshua, much as God did Abraham and Moses: to lead Israel to the promised land. The crossing over that Joshua is called to lead is symbolic in many ways. The ark of the covenant was understood to be the symbolic representation of God's presence with the people and was said to contain the original tablets of the commandments given to Moses.

In the times of the Hebrew scriptures, land was the sign of a fulfilled life, signifying happiness and contentment. Societal order relied heavily on land, not just for material wealth but also as a sign of spiritual well being. Just as the gift of land was evidence of God's favor, the crossing of the waters holds great significance for Israel as evidence of being the redeemed people of God. (A similar example is found in the Exodus account of the crossing of the Red Sea.) The portrayal of the crossing is ritualistic in nature, and the event has been reenacted during Passover by stopping the Jordan with locks placed at the points described in the account so people could cross the dry riverbed.

The crossing of the Jordan is a story of power and promise. The monument of twelve stones commemorates God's power more than the accomplishments of Joshua. The crossing of the river symbolizes a renewed conquest authority under Joshua: Israel was marching toward Jericho and victory. Violence is a part of this legacy. The Israelites were headed into battle because the promised land was not vacant but was inhabited by Canaanites. God promised to Joshua absolute protection as the people of Israel took over this land.

While the Hebrew scriptures do have a theme of Israel as the chosen people, it has another consistent theme—that all creation is united under God. With the benefit of historical hindsight, we might wonder how different global reality might be if the second great theme had been more prominent than the first. Perhaps it is not too late to emphasize the oneness of humanity.

PUSH OUT

- Create a memory box or book that commemorates a special time in your life by collecting relevant cards, pictures, rocks, drawings, pamphlets, coasters, and other items. For each event include one page of your own writing on why that event is so important to you and how you felt during that time. Share the contents of your memory box with others.

- Discover more of your story by finding out how your family came to the place it is now. There are numerous genealogy sites on the Internet to help you go more in-depth into your family history.

- Volunteer at a nursing home or visit with older people in your church and interview them, collecting their stories. Create memory boxes with them. Keep them in a church library for others to learn from in later generations. Help pass the story on.

- Create a monument that encourages peace and reconciliation. Perhaps plant a tree or install a Peace Pole. Information about Peace Poles can be found at <www.worldpeace.org/activities>. Create a worship service around the dedication of the monument.

- Examine your country's colonial history by conducting a discussion or study group. Visit monuments in your community that commemorate colonization. Endeavor to meet with First Nations peoples and hear their stories. Bring history up-to-date by reading the news for stories about the business dealings of developed countries in developing countries. Where do you see history repeating itself? Where are new legacies of peace and interdependence being created?

- Study the historic relationship between Israel and Palestine. One place to begin might be <www.mideastweb.org/briefhistory>.

GROUP IDEAS

[Focus: To make heritage out of history.

LIFE'S A PUSH

- Try to meet by the water. Have a pile of stones available where you will congregate. If that is not possible, place a large bowl of water with river stones in the bottom in the center of your meeting space. (Stones can be purchased at floral or craft stores if they are not readily available in your area.)

- Read aloud the "Life's a Push" section on pages 35–36, then give the group time to write their version of a family story incorporating their "stones." Allow the group to share with each other some of their writings.

- Engage the questions provided on page 36.

THE STORY

- As alternating voices read the scripture on page 38, invite all who are able to walk in a circle. At the close of the scripture, have each person from the group take a stone. Then have everyone sit in a circle and share one story about one of their "tribes," which could be friends, family, band mates, or others. After they are finished, have them place their stone back in the center to create some sort of collective commemoration of the tribes represented.

YOU PUSH THE STORY

- Consider the "Push Possibilities" for Joshua 3:7–8; 3:14—4:8 on page 39.

- Allow the group to add their own pushes.

THE STORY PUSHES YOU

- Explore the "Push Possibilities" on page 39 as a group.

PUSH OUT

- Have the group plan a type of monument they would like to create after participating in one of the study ideas suggested in the "Push Out" section on page 41. Involve the larger community in the dedication of the monument.

- Choose other push outs to do together as a group or to do individually and share with the group later.

- Close with a prayer of thanksgiving for memories and heritage. Include petitions for healing and restoration for those who have suffered from legacies of oppression.

3. [PEACEMAKING IN A VIOLENT WORLD

David said to Abigail, "Blessed be the Lord, the God of Israel, who sent you to meet me today! Blessed be your good sense, and blessed be you, who have kept me today from bloodguilt and from avenging myself by my own blood."

1 Samuel 25:32

Have you ever helped someone else resist the impulse to get even? How might God be calling you to be a peacemaker in a violent world?

 LIFE'S A PUSH

DO SOMETHING

Richard Rhodes, Pulitzer Prize winner for his 1986 book *The Making of the Atomic Bomb* (New York: Simon & Schuster, 1986), lost his mother to suicide when he was thirteen months old. He was ten when his father remarried. Richard's stepmother turned out to be as cruel as the worst folklore stepmothers.

For two-and-a-half years, Rhodes and his brother were abused—kicked, beaten, denied baths and showers, and deliberately starved. In his autobiographical book, *A Hole in the World: An American Boyhood* (New York: Simon & Schuster, 1990), he writes, "I've often wondered how my brother and I survived with our capacity to love intact. I always come back to the same answer—strangers helped us."

Strangers helped them. In the face of cruelty and abuse, strangers helped them. Rhodes learned something very important from those early experiences. He learned that doing nothing in the face of evil allows evil to happen. "Don't be a bystander," he says in the autobiography, "Do something."

Read below a poem by Marge Piercy in which she describes people of action:

> The people I love the best
> jump into work headfirst
> without dallying in the shallows
> and swim off with sure strokes almost out of sight.
> They seem to become natives of that element,
> the black sleek heads of seals
> bouncing like half-submerged balls.

I love people who harness themselves, an ox to a heavy cart,
who pull like water buffalo, with massive patience,
who strain in the mud and the muck to move things forward,
who do what has to be done, again and again.

I want to be with people who submerge
in the task, who go into the fields to harvest
and work in a row and pass the bags along,
who are not parlor generals and field deserters
but move in a common rhythm
when the food must come in or the fire put out.

The work of the world is common as mud,
botched, it smears the hands, crumbles to dust.
But the thing worth doing well done
has a shape that satisfies, clean and evident.
Greek amphoras for wine or oil,
Hopi vases that held corn, are put in museums
but you know they were made to be used.
The pitcher cries for water to carry
and a person for work that is real.[1]

- How does Piercy's poem make you feel? What images stand out most for you in the poem?

- Do you know of people who are always there when "the food must come in or the fire put out"?

- What are examples of "work that is real"?

TIKKUN OLAM

There is a Jewish tradition named *tikkun olam*—mending the world. Arthur Green, author of *Seek My Face, Speak My Name* (Jason Aronson, Northvale, NJ, 1992) which explores new metaphors for God within Judaism, describes it this way: "In contemporary usage it refers to the betterment of the world, including the relief of human suffering, the achievement of peace and mutual respect among peoples, and the protection of the planet itself from destruction."[2]

- Name people or places in the news where there is abuse, injustice, neglect, or wrongdoing. How do you feel, act, and respond when you are confronted with these issues?

■ When have you practiced *tikkun olam* in your life? How might you incorporate the practice into your work or your choice of future work? into your free time and social time with friends and groups?

PRAYER

Breathe in and out deeply as you pray this portion of the prayer of St. Francis several times in succession: "Lord, make me an instrument of your peace."

THE STORY

Read the story in 1 Samuel 25:2–39, 42b. As you read, try imagining that you are Abigail. What does the story feel like from her perspective? Choose a way to experience the story from the Bible Experience ideas on pages 17–23.

²There was a man in Maon, whose property was in Carmel. The man was very rich; he had three thousand sheep and a thousand goats. He was shearing his sheep in Carmel. ³Now the name of the man was Nabal, and the name of his wife Abigail. The woman was clever and beautiful, but the man was surly and mean; he was a Calebite. ⁴David heard in the wilderness that Nabal was shearing his sheep. ⁵So David sent ten young men; and David said to the young men, "Go up to Carmel, and go to Nabal, and greet him in my name. ⁶Thus you shall salute him: 'Peace be to you, and peace be to your house, and peace be to all that you have. ⁷I hear that you have shearers; now your shepherds have been with us, and we did them no harm, and they missed nothing, all the time they were in Carmel. ⁸Ask your young men, and they will tell you. Therefore let my young men find favor in your sight; for we have come on a feast day. Please give whatever you have at hand to your servants and to your son David.'"

⁹When David's young men came, they said all this to Nabal in the name of David; and then they waited. ¹⁰But Nabal answered David's servants, "Who is David? Who is the son of Jesse? There are many servants today who are breaking away from their masters. ¹¹Shall I take my bread and my water and the meat that I have butchered for my shearers, and give it to men who come from I do not know where?" ¹²So David's young men turned away, and came back and told him all this. ¹³David said to his men, "Every man strap on his sword!" And every one of them

strapped on his sword; David also strapped on his sword; and about four hundred men went up after David, while two hundred remained with the baggage.

[14]But one of the young men told Abigail, Nabal's wife, "David sent messengers out of the wilderness to salute our master; and he shouted insults at them. [15]Yet the men were very good to us, and we suffered no harm, and we never missed anything when we were in the fields, as long as we were with them; [16]they were a wall to us both by night and by day, all the while we were with them keeping the sheep. [17]Now therefore know this and consider what you should do; for evil has been decided against our master and against all his house; he is so ill-natured that no one can speak to him."

[18]Then Abigail hurried and took two hundred loaves, two skins of wine, five sheep ready dressed, five measures of parched grain, one hundred clusters of raisins, and two hundred cakes of figs. She loaded them on donkeys and said to her young men, "Go on ahead of me; I am coming after you." But she did not tell her husband Nabal. [20]As she rode on the donkey and came down under cover of the mountain, David and his men came down toward her; and she met them. [21]Now David had said, "Surely it was in vain that I protected all that this fellow has in the wilderness, so that nothing was missed of all that belonged to him; but he has returned me evil for good. [22]God do so to David and more also, if by morning I leave so much as one male of all who belong to him."

[23]When Abigail saw David, she hurried and alighted from the donkey, and fell before David on her face, bowing to the ground. [24]She fell at his feet and said, "Upon me alone, my lord, be the guilt; please let your servant speak in your ears, and hear the words of your servant. [25]My lord, do not take seriously this ill-natured fellow, Nabal; for as his name is, so is he; Nabal is his name, and folly is with him; but I, your servant did not see the young men of my lord, whom you sent.

[26]Now then, my lord, as the Lord lives, and as you yourself live, since the Lord has restrained you from bloodguilt and from taking vengeance with your own hand, now let your enemies and those who see to do evil to my lord be like Nabal. [27]And now let this present that your servant has brought to my lord be given to the young men who follow my lord. [28]Please forgive the trespass of your servant; for the Lord will certainly make my lord a sure house, because my lord is fighting the battles of the Lord; and evil shall not be found in you so long as you live. [29]If anyone should rise up to pursue you and to seek your life, the life of my lord shall be bound in the bundle of the living under the care of the

Lord your God; but the lives of your enemies he shall sling out as from the hollow of a sling. [30]When the Lord has done to my lord according to all the good that he has spoken concerning you, and has appointed you prince over Israel, my lord shall have no cause of grief, or pangs of conscience, for having shed blood without cause or for having saved himself. And when the Lord has dealt well with my lord, then remember your servant."

[32]David said to Abigail, "Blessed be the Lord, the God of Israel, who sent you to meet me today! Blessed be your good sense, and blessed be you, who have kept me today from bloodguilt and from avenging myself by my own hand! [34]For as surely as the Lord the God of Israel lives, who has restrained me from hurting you, unless you hurried and came to meet me, truly by morning there would not have been left to Nabal so much as one male." [35]Then David received from her hand what she had brought him; he said to her, "Go up to your house in peace; see, I have heeded your voice, and I have granted your petition."

[36]Abigail came to Nabal; he was holding a feast in his house, like the feast of a king. Nabal's heart was merry within him, for he was very drunk; so she told him nothing at all until the morning light. [37]In the morning, when the wine had gone out of Nabal, his wife told him these things, and his heart died within him; he became like a stone. [38]About ten days later the Lord struck Nabal, and he died.

[39]When David heard that Nabal was dead, he said, "Blessed be the Lord who has judged the case of Nabal's insult to me, and has kept back his servant from evil; the Lord has returned the evildoing of Nabal upon his own head." Then David sent and wooed Abigail, to make her his wife. . . . [42b]She went after the messengers of David and became his wife.

YOU PUSH THE STORY

What stands out for you in this story? Have you come across Abigail before or is her story new to you? How do you react to David's threat to kill all the men in Nabal's household? Does Abigail's swift response to David's threat surprise you? What other reactions do you have to the story? Review "The Story Behind the Story" on pages 48–49 for some background information.

PUSH POSSIBILITIES FOR 1 SAMUEL 25:2–39, 42B

- The three main actors in this story—Nabal, David, and Abigail—reflect very different character traits. How would you describe each of them?

- What males belong to Nabal? What makes David so angry as to want to kill them all?
- What is bloodguilt and why is it so important to David that he be kept from it?
- Why did one of Nabal's men go to Abigail with information about David?
- What provokes Abigail to respond to the situation?
- Why does Abigail agree to marry David?
- Why does the story seem so much like a fairy tale?

THE STORY PUSHES YOU

What does this story challenge us to reflect on? What does the story challenge us to do? How does it push us to rethink our lives and the impact of our actions on the world?

PUSH POSSIBILITIES FOR 1 SAMUEL 25:2–39, 42B

- What is "work that is real" in the context of this passage?
- Think about the challenge the story has for you in your life right now. Are you like Nabal—a fool given over to ingratitude and rudeness? Are you like David—a powerful leader, quick to judge, and dismissive of dissenters? Are you like Abigail—a peacemaker committed to doing justice regardless of the risks?
- What provokes you to act for peace and justice?
- In *The Imitation of Christ*, Thomas à Kempis writes, "Keep yourself at peace first, and then you will be able to bring peace to others. A person who is at peace with himself [herself] does more good than someone who is very learned."[3] How do you practice peace?

THE STORY BEHIND THE STORY

This story introduces Abigail, one of the most intriguing women of the Bible. She is given a leading role and acts on her own initiative, a real surprise in the midst of such a patriarchal society. Her description is quite full, also rare in the scriptures, which often do not even name women. We are told of her gifts of intelligence, beauty, and resourcefulness, gifts that are put to good use and God's purposes in this story of her encounter with David.

Abigail's husband Nabal, however, is her polar opposite. He is not intelligent, handsome, or resourceful. In fact Nabal (whose name means "fool") is vicious, obnoxious, and ungrateful. He is so mean-spirited that even his servants say he is "so ill-natured that no one can speak to him." What sort of person, the story asks, would refuse a request for hospitality from a man who has six hundred armed men with him? Nabal would have been required by social code to provide hospitality to David or any other travelers, but he was even more obliged to David for having used this army to protect Nabal's shepherds. David's anger was to an extent understandable, although his reaction of planning to kill everyone who had anything to do with Nabal was extreme.

Enter Abigail. It is interesting to note that the servants would come to her directly, again highlighting her abilities and gifts. Abigail is not content simply to send food to David. She sets out to meet him herself and becomes personally involved. Her words and demeanor so impress David that he immediately accepts her gifts and sends her home in peace.

A primary purpose of the story is to demonstrate David's character as the future king of Israel (at this point in his story he is still on the run from the current king, Saul, who recognizes David's growing power and would like nothing more than to extinguish this threat to his crown). Here David demonstrates a willingness to practice restraint concerning violence. As we know from later stories, David will not always be so restrained. (See the story of David and Uriah the Hittite, whom David has killed in order to take his wife Bethsheba for himself in 2 Samuel 11.)

Clearly David also demonstrates in this story that he is a savvy political operator: wiping out such a prominent family as Nabal's would have made it much more difficult for him to ascend to the throne. He actually ends up developing an alliance with the family through his marriage to Abigail.

The main purpose of the story is to show how God is at work among the people and that God's plans will be fulfilled. This theme is most dramatically sounded in Nabal's death, which is attributed to God. It is also clearly woven into the story of Abigail, however, who uses her gifts to enable God's purposes.

PUSH OUT

"Don't be a bystander. Do something."

- What practices—prayer, silence, journaling—might deepen your own personal well of peace from which to draw for the healing of this world? It might be something as simple as starting each day with a prayer, asking God to give you a peaceful spirit. You might covenant with a close friend to do this, each of you on your own during the week and together on a weekend morning. Print a short prayer for peace—St. Francis's words, "Let me be an instrument of thy peace" or "Keep me peaceful, keep me mindful of you"—on an index card and carry it in your pocket or in your daily planner notebook. Every time you come across the card, repeat your prayer.

- There are some deeply moving Web sites that are good sources of peace and prayer for you throughout the day. Christ in the Desert Monastery in New Mexico offers daily prayers, chants, and artwork for deepening spirituality. Their address is <www.christdesert.org>. The Jesuits in Ireland host a site called Sacred Space located at <www.jesuit.ie/prayer/>. You'll find a simple prayer process you can engage in right at your computer. There is a powerful collection of world prayers at <www.worldprayers.org>. From the site <www.worldprayers.org/bookmark>you can add a bookmark to your computer that will give you quick access to invocations and other prayers and meditations anytime you want. Denominational Web sites such as the United Church of Christ's offer resources for prayer and peacemaking. Their address is <www.ucc.org/justice/index.html>. Or check the home pages of other denominations in the United States and Canada for similar information.

No matter what spiritual practices you choose, remember to be gentle with yourself. Peacemaking takes time, whether it's peacemaking inside your heart or outside in the world.

- What skills of yours lend themselves to repairing the world? What kind of time do you give to helping and healing others? Start a "peacemaking journal." Look back over the past few years, taking note of some of the things you've done that count as peacemaking. In the weeks ahead, write down situations you come across where you can do or say something that will make for peace. Ask others what they see in your character and personality that might be natural avenues for peacemaking. Reflect in your journal on what they say. What does your journal suggest about future directions and actions for peacemaking in your life?

- What organizations are working in your neighborhood or community to bring peace? What can you do to help these organizations?

- Make a commitment to do something to help bring healing and joy to the people who are your neighbors—those in your family, in your neighborhood, or halfway around the world. Volunteer. Write to government officials. Run errands for someone who is sick or shut-in. Speak up when you hear people around you denigrate others. Adopt an endangered species or a threatened ecosystem. Devote one Saturday a month to an ongoing political cause, neighborhood issue, or local project. One day at a time—one small corner of the world at a time—one piece at a time—one peace at a time.

GROUP IDEAS

[

Focus: To gain insight into what it means to be called by God to be a peacemaker in a violent world.

LIFE'S A PUSH

- Bring in magazine and newspaper photos and headlines of trouble spots in the world. These could be local, statewide, national, or global issues. Post them on a bulletin board or on poster board in a place where the group can see them as they enter.

- Read the short reflection about Richard Rhodes on page 43. Allow people to react to Rhodes's situation as a boy and to his exhortation to act.

- Read Marge Piercy's poem, "To Be of Use," on pages 43–44. Have one person in the group read it aloud. Then ask another person to read it aloud a second time. Spend some time talking about the images Piercy uses, and ask people to talk about what feelings the poem evokes. Discuss the reflection questions on page 44.

- Discuss the tradition of *tikkun olam* and the reflection questions on page 45.

- Lead the breathing prayer using the portion of the prayer of St. Francis that is provided on page 45.

THE STORY

- Use background material from "The Story Behind the Story" on pages 48–49 to introduce the group to the passage from 1 Samuel 25:2–39, 42b.

- Distribute pieces of clay to the group and invite participants to work with it during the reading. Read the story aloud together as readers' theatre, asking one group member to be the narrator, one to be Nabal, one to be David, one to be Nabal's servants, and one to be Abigail. Have group members share their experiences of playing these roles. What parts of the story frightened them? What parts inspired them? What were they inspired to create in clay as they listened?

YOU PUSH THE STORY

- Ask the group what they know from the Bible about David. What stories do they associate with him? What is his reputation as a young boy? as a young man? as a king in Israel? Have people read the following for more of a picture of David: the story of David and Goliath in 1 Samuel 17; David's friendship with Jonathan reflecting David's character in 1 Samuel 18:1–5 and 1 Samuel 23:16–18; David's superior abilities as a king shown in his military successes and his expansion of the kingdom through the acquisition of land in 2 Samuel 8, 10, 11; and David as an adulterous husband (2 Samuel 11:1—12:25) and as a doting father (2 Samuel 13:34–39).

■ Discuss reactions to David's being so quick to anger and then so ready to accept peace. Are there other great men and women in history whose character—and character flaws—remind group members of David?

■ Engage the push possibilities on page 48.

THE STORY PUSHES YOU

■ Ask group members to reflect on the story in terms of their lives. Given where they are right now and what is going on in their lives, which character most pushes them? Nabal's attitude of ingratitude, Abigail's radical risk-taking, David's petulant power trip, or his acceptance of Abigail's gift—which of these most characterize where people in the group are today? What are they learning from these characters about how they would like to be in the future?

■ Invite the group to work with the push possibilities on page 48.

PUSH OUT

■ Have the group talk about ways to address both the inner-peacemaking and the outer-peacemaking suggestions on pages 49–50. Commit to one or two of the ideas as a group.

■ Close with prayer. You might pray a circle prayer, asking each member of the group in turn to lift up some place in the world that needs peace or some people in the world who are working for peace. Aloud or silently, lift up the needs each individual has in her or his own life for peace. Ask God to guide each individual and the group toward responding to God's call to "mend the world."

1.   Marge Piercy, "To Be of Use," *Circles on the Water* (New York: Albert A. Knopf, 1982), 106. Used by permission.

2.   Arthur Green, "Words Matter: *Tikkun Olam*," <www.socialaction.com/wordsmatter.html>.

3.   Thomas à Kempis, *The Imitation of Christ in Four Books: A Translation from the Latin* (Vintage Books, 1998), Translated by Joseph N. Tylenda, Revised Edition.

4. [WHEN A LAW IS NOT THE LAW

All . . . agreed that the king should establish an ordinance and enforce an interdict that whoever prays to anyone, human or divine, for thirty days, except to you, O King, shall be thrown into a den of lions. Although Daniel knew that the document had been signed, he continued to go to his house . . . and to get down on his knees three times a day to pray to his God and praise him, just as he had always done.

Daniel 6:7, 10

At times, our faith calls us out into the open to bear public witness for justice.

IFE'S A PUSH

DISOBEYING DEATH

He made his fortune through contacts with his fellow Nazis. He used the cheapest form of labor possible at the time, persecuted Jews. Nevertheless, Oscar Schindler decided to risk all that he had to save "his" twelve hundred Jews—mothers, sons, grandchildren—from slaughter. Although his workers were forced to live in the Plaszow labor camp, Schindler convinced the commandant to move them into their own sub-camp. Schindler smuggled food and medicine in to them. Twice he was arrested for these efforts. He spent every night at his factory in his office to make sure the Gestapo didn't enter. He even manipulated his records to protect the workers, knocking years off the ages of each of the older workers and registering children as adults. Schindler listed doctors and lawyers as factory workers and mechanics, since these were the only jobs that needed to be filled. By the end of the war he had spent his entire fortune on saving the people who worked for him.

When the German army began experiencing losses, Plaszow was marked for closure. Death was the only fate that awaited its occupants. Schindler went to Berlin to save his workers from certain annihilation—begging, bribing, and bullying until he was given permission to move his factory to Czechoslovakia and to take his workers with him. Three hundred of the women were sent by error to Auschwitz where they were to be killed. After several weeks they were herded toward the showers, not knowing if there would be water or gas. As they approached the showers, Schindler's voice rang out, demanding to know what

53

was happening to the women. The women were released—the only prisoners to leave Auschwitz during its entire history as a death camp.

After the war, Schindler was threatened by former Nazis, deprived of his nationality, and denied entry to the United States because he had been a member of the Nazi party. He fled to Argentina, where thankful members of the Jewish community financially supported him.

At great personal risk and loss, Oscar Schindler stood up to the law of the land. Perhaps he was responding to a higher law.

TAKING A STAND

During the 1970s and early 1980s in Argentina, more than thirty thousand people were "made to disappear." They were victims of that nation's brutal military dictatorship, kidnapped or arrested, often with no charges or warning. Families were left without explanation, without information, and with no way to appeal. In those years of fear and oppression, when to protest could well mean joining the ranks of the "disappeared," mothers of many who had been taken began to gather in public places holding pictures of those who were missing. They demanded answers. Still gathering today, particularly at the Plaza de Mayo in Buenos Aires, these mothers wear white shawls symbolic of Catholic motherhood and hold their placards in silent protest. The Mothers of Plaza de Mayo have grown to become one of the world's most remarkable protest and justice movements. For more than twenty years they have gathered on the plaza every week. They have also begun a free university for people who want to work for justice.

IT'S NOT JUST FOR MOTHERS ANYMORE

Here is a story about another group who decided to take a stand, taken from a Web site about the history of the Raging Grannies protest organization:

> The original Raging Grannies group formed in Victoria, B.C., in February 1987 when a group of eight women, worried about nuclear proliferation and particularly the danger of nuclear-powered and nuclear-armed vessels coming into Canadian waters, decided to get their message across by singing protest songs. Then they decided to target other abuses of society, such as environmental and social concerns. Success came quickly, and other groups sprang up across Canada in Toronto, Ottawa, Montreal, Kamloops, and Halifax. Groups continue to form across Canada and may soon start in the United States as well.

TAKING A SEAT

The date was February 1, 1960, and the place was Greensboro, North Carolina. Businesses were allowed to exclude African Americans from any part of their operations, such as sitting in certain sections of the establishments, using the facilities, or making purchases at various times of the day. That February day, four African American college students decided it was time to take a stand. So they sat down. They sat in the "whites only" section at the counter of a Woolworth's store and ordered coffee, donuts, and sodas. They were told they would not be served.

And they weren't. But they stayed seated there until the store closed that evening. The students, who came to be known as the Greensboro Four, returned the next day and the next, each day joined by more and more people in more and more restaurants. The sit-in went on for five months before the Woolworth's store manager agreed to integrate. The struggle to change the laws that sanctioned segregation continued for years to come.

- What do you think motivates people to protest laws or regulations?

- How do you understand the relationship, if you think there is any, between God's will and human laws?

- Do you think religious beliefs play a role in guiding an individual's life in society? If so, how?

- Imagine being in any one of the situations described in this section. What internal resources would you draw upon to face the risks these others faced?

- What would Jesus do in these situations? What are followers of Jesus called to do in these situations?

- What are the many aspects of situations like these that need to be considered?

PRAYER

God of Life
prepare our hands for a touch
a new and different touch
prepare our hands for a touch
a touch of encounter
a touch of awakening
a touch of hope
a touch of feeling
Many are the worn-out gestures
many are the movements frozen in time
Many are the useless excuses just to repeat attitudes . . .
Give us daring
to create new titles of community
new links of affection
breaking away from old ways of relating,
encouraging true, meaningful ways to move into closeness.[1]

THE STORY

Have someone tell the story from Daniel 6:6–23. You may want to choose a method of sharing the story from the Bible Experience ideas on page 23.

⁶So the presidents ands satraps conspired and came to the king and said to him, "O King Darius, live forever! ⁷All the presidents of the kingdom, the prefects and the satraps, the counselors and the governors are agreed that the king should establish an ordinance and enforce an interdict, that whoever prays to anyone, divine or human, for thirty days, except to you, O King, shall be thrown into a den of lions. ⁸Now, O King, establish the interdict and sign the document, so that it cannot be changed, according to the law of the Medes and the Persians, which cannot be revoked." ⁹Therefore King Darius signed the document and interdict.

¹⁰Although Daniel knew that the document had been signed, he continued to go to his house, which had windows in its upper room open toward Jerusalem, and to get down on his knees three times a day to pray to his God and praise him, just as he had done previously. ¹¹The conspirators came and found Daniel praying and seeking mercy before his God. ¹²Then they approached the king and said concerning the interdict, "Oh King! Did you not sign an interdict, that anyone who prays to anyone, divine or human, within thirty days except to you, O King, shall be thrown into a den of lions?" The king answered, "The thing stands fast, according to the law of the Medes and Persians, which cannot be revoked." ¹³Then they responded to the king, "Daniel, one of the exiles from Judah, pays no attention to you, O King, or to the interdict you have signed, but he is saying his prayers three times a day."

¹⁴When the king heard the charge, he was very much distressed. He was determined to save Daniel, and until the sun went down he made every effort to rescue him. ¹⁵Then the conspirators came to the king and said to him, "Know, O King, that it is a law of the Medes and Persians that no interdict or ordinance that the king establishes can be changed."

¹⁶Then the king gave the command, and Daniel was brought and thrown into the den of lions. The king said to Daniel, "May your God, whom you faithfully serve, deliver you!" ¹⁷A stone was brought and laid on the mouth of the den, and the king sealed it with his own signet and with the signet of his lords, so that nothing might be changed concerning Daniel. ¹⁸Then the king went to his palace and spent the night fasting; no food was brought to him, and sleep fled from him.

¹⁹Then, at the break of day, the king got up and hurried to the den of lions. ²⁰When he came near the den where Daniel was, he cried out

anxiously to Daniel, "O Daniel, servant of the living God, has your God whom you faithfully serve been able to deliver you from the lions?"

²¹Daniel then said to the king, "O King, live forever! ²²My God sent his angel and shut the lions' mouths so that they would not hurt me, because I was found blameless before him; and also before you, O king, I have done no wrong." ²³Then the king was exceedingly glad and commanded that Daniel be taken up out of he den. So Daniel was taken up out of the den, and no kind of harm was found on him, because he had trusted in his God.

YOU PUSH THE STORY

Perhaps you know this story, or parts of it, or the general sense of it from the way it's referred to in our culture so often. What new insights come to you from reading the entire story? What questions emerge? One way to push a story like this is to think about the motives of the characters. Only the satraps seem transparent—jealousy is obviously fueling their fires. Add your own questions to the following pushes.

PUSH POSSIBILITIES FOR DANIEL 6:6–23

- How can the king be so oscillating—going along with the satraps one minute and trying to save Daniel from his own decree the next?
- Why does Daniel pray in front of open windows?
- What "law of God" was Daniel observing in his three-times-daily prayers?
- Does the king convert to Daniel's beliefs?
- How might others have responded to the decree? What about Daniel's family and community? How might they have reacted to Daniel?

THE STORY PUSHES YOU

These questions can begin your thinking about how the story pushes you.

PUSH POSSIBILITIES FOR DANIEL 6:6–23

- Have you ever operated out of fear or jealousy?
- Is there a right or wrong place and time for public display of faith or religion?
- Have you ever found yourself compromising your own values or beliefs in order to keep the peace?

■ As a way to entrap Jesus, religious leaders asked him about paying taxes. (See Matthew 22:15–22, Mark 12:13–17, or Luke 20:20–26.) Jesus responds by saying, "Give therefore to the emperor the things that are the emperor's and to God the things that are God's" (Matthew 22:21). How does this response relate to Daniel's story?

THE STORY BEHIND THE STORY

This story is set in the time of the Babylonian exile. Babylonian armies routinely sent the intellectual, political, and social elite of conquered countries to Babylon, leaving the general population of the conquered country without leadership. While this allowed for a cosmopolitan and diverse leadership pool in the Babylonian cities, it also set up ready opportunities for jealousy among the local leadership when exiles rose through the ranks into positions of power. This is what had happened in Daniel's case. Chapter 6:1–6 sets the stage by reporting that the king planned to set Daniel over all the other satraps, or high officials. The local leadership appealed to the king to help rid themselves of Daniel, having the king sign a decree that was irrevocable. This custom of immutable laws among the Medes and Persians is attested to in Esther 1:19 and 8:8, as well as by some Greek authors.

Daniel follows the practice of praying three times daily at a window facing toward the temple in Jerusalem as prescribed by the Talmudic law (instructions based on God's given laws) and referred to in some Psalms. While he is not praying publicly to incite a problem, neither is he backing down from his usual practice just because of the new edict.

A problem is created for the nation, however. Conquering empires routinely used conversion to their own religion as a tool of control. Daniel's insistence on the public practice of his faith was a destabilizing influence, particularly in light of his prominent position.

Scholars have long speculated on the symbolism of the lions in this story. Early writers believed they represented the underworld. In the psalms the lions are symbolic of chaos (Psalm 91:13). It has also been suggested that they are a metaphor for the exile.

It should be noted that Darius the Mede is not a historically identifiable figure. Some scholars argue that the book of Daniel was written during the reign of Antiochus IV, a truly ferocious and capricious ruler. Although the stories are of another time and place, they tell readers how to behave under the domination of a foreign power, reminding the people that if they are faithful to God, God will be faithful to them.

PUSH OUT

There is sometimes a tension between the demands for justice inherent in the Christian faith and the laws of the land. How do we respond faithfully? Use these ideas as ways to explore your own beliefs and ideas.

- Learn more about the Mothers of Plaza de Mayo at their Web site <www.madres.org>. Available in Spanish only.

- The movie *Gandhi* (RCA/Columbia Home Video; dir. Richard Attenborough, 1982) gives helpful definition to the reality of unjust laws. Martin Luther King Jr.'s book *Stride Toward Freedom* (New York: Harper & Row, 1958) and his "Letter from a Birmingham Jail" do as well.

- Watch the movie *Philadelphia.* (Columbia TriStar Home Videos; dir. Jonathan Demme, 1993) What are your reactions to the laws that are challenged in the movie? What do you notice about what motivates the characters who either uphold or challenge the laws? Try to place yourself in the movie. Which character do you relate to most according to your faith and values?

- Are there specific laws or regulations that you feel do not measure up to God's hope for creation? How can you become involved in changes around these issues? You might start with correspondence with government officials. Express your views and ask for their opinions and commitments in return. For contact information, go to:

  United States   www.congress.org
  Canada   http://canada.gc.ca

- Daniel's commitment to prayer was not the only reason for his getting into trouble; it was the reason he was able to get through the trouble. Assess your own prayer routine. Is prayer a part of your daily life?

- An excellent example of fighting for civil rights from within the U.S. would be the women's movement of the mid-to-late-nineteenth century, the suffragettes, and the women's movement that began in the late 1960s. The nineteenth-century group was part of the abolitionists who fought for an end to slavery. Because they were silenced in the public sphere by their male colleagues, women realized that being denied the right to vote also denied them a voice. Their tireless efforts against the injustice of laws that prohibited women from voting—including attempting to vote in elections across the country—was not realized during the lifetime of Lucretia Mott, Elizabeth Cady Stanton, or even Susan B. Anthony. It was 1920—less than a century ago—when women in the United States were given the right to vote, when

Tennessee ratified the Nineteenth Amendment. For more information and a brief history, see <http://womenshistory.about.com/cs/suffrage/>. These women also fought for the rights of married women, for laws to protect those who were abused, and for money to build shelters for them. Such fights were continued by the women's movement in the late-twentieth century as laws were made that prohibited husbands from legally raping and physically assaulting their wives, practices that had been considered part of a husband's authority. Consider a trip to the United States Women's Rights National Historical Park in Seneca Falls, New York, or go to <www.nps.gov/wori/wrnhp.htm> on the Web.

For information about current work in the area of human rights for women, visit the Women's Human Rights Resources Web site of the Bora Laskin Law Library at the University of Toronto at <www.law-lib.utoronto.ca/diana/>.

- Get involved—or get your mother or your grandmother involved—in the Raging Grannies movement in Canada and the United States. Information can be found at <www.raginggrannies.com/history.html>.

GROUP IDEAS [Focus: To examine the role of faith in the public sphere, particularly in challenging injustice.

LIFE'S A PUSH

- Obtain copies of any of several books or articles about resistance to the Nazi movement. These could include *The Hiding Place* by Corrie ten Boom (New York; Toronto: Bantam, 1971), *Schindler's Ark* by Thomas Keneally (London: Hodder & Stoughton, 1982), or *The Diary of Anne Frank*. Suggest that several members each take something to read. Pierre Sauvage's one-hour video documentary *Weapons of the Spirit: A Documentary* (Los Angeles: Friends of Le Chambon Foundation, 1989) attempts to understand why the entire population of Le Chambon-sur-Lignon defied the laws of the land and saved over five thousand Jews from the death camps because "it was the only thing to do." If at all possible, make this film available for viewing by the group.

- Read the vignettes on pages 53–55 and discuss the issues raised. If the group is large, break into smaller groups and have each group work with one of the stories.

- Allow group members some silent time to sort out some of their own feelings about these issues, then read together the prayer on page 55 or pray one of your own.

THE STORY

- Do a dramatic reading of the Biblical passage on page 56–57 together, with different people reading the lines of the various characters and narrator.

YOU PUSH THE STORY

- Ask a participant to read "The Story Behind the Story" on page 58.

- Ask the group members to select from the push possibilities on page 57 the things they would like to discuss or to come up with their own questions.

THE STORY PUSHES YOU

- Encourage members to relate any personal experiences that are suggested by the push possibilities on pages 57–58.

PUSH OUT

- Be prepared with some of the resources suggested on pages 59–60. Ask the group to decide on one or two of these ideas that they would like to do or come up with others.

- The entire text of the outstanding meditation aide *The Practice of the Presence of God* by Brother Lawrence (1611–1691) is available online at <www.ccel.org/l/lawrence/practice/htm> or copies can be obtained at most Christian bookstores. Arrange for the members of the group to have access to this piece and encourage them to begin or enhance their private meditation time with it. Or suggest other materials that you think might be helpful for them.

- Offer the following closing prayer or one of your own:

PRAYER

Holy God, thank you for your presence in all parts of our lives. Let us be open to seeing you and knowing you. Help us to not be afraid to question what is in the light of what should be. Amen.

1. Ernesto Barros Cardoso, "Gathering Words and Invocations," *Gifts of Many Cultures*, ed. Maren C. Tirabassi and Kathy Wonson Eddy (Cleveland: United Church Press, 1995), 4.

5 [LETTING IT GO

When God saw what [the Ninevites] did, how they
turned from their evil ways, God changed his mind
about the calamity that he had said he would bring
upon them; and he did not do it. But this was very
displeasing to Jonah, and he became angry.

Jonah 3:10—4:1

> What would it mean for our communities if we
> were angry at injustice but compassionate towards
> people?

LIFE'S A PUSH

FULL OF ANGER

Frederick Buechner offers an interesting spin on anger. In *Wishful Thinking: A
Theological ABC* (New York, Harper & Row, 1973) he writes, "Of the Seven
Deadly Sins, anger is possibly the most fun. To lick your wounds, to smack your
lips over grievances long past, to roll over your tongue the prospect of bitter con-
frontations still to come, to savor to the last toothsome morsel both the pain you
are given and the pain you are giving back—in many ways it is a feast fit for a
king. The chief drawback is that what you are wolfing down is yourself. The
skeleton at the feast is you."

- How do you respond to this viewpoint?
- Do you know people who seem to feast on anger? What is your experience of
  them?

A BALM FOR ALL WOUNDS

Etty Hillesum was a young Jewish woman who was imprisoned in the Auschwitz
death camp during the Holocaust. Etty was described by those who knew her as
a "luminous personality." Her journals, published in the 1980s as *An Interrupted
Life* (New York: Pantheon, 1983), reveal the hope and joy she had in her work,
in her friendships, and in her relationship with God, even as World War II
encroached with its cruelty, suffering and, finally, with her murder in the camp.

Jan Richardson in her book *In Wisdom's Path: Discovering the Sacred in Every
Season* (Cleveland: The Pilgrim Press, 2000) says this of Etty: "With her words

and with her life, Etty bore stunning witness to the terror of the times, to her belief in the exquisiteness of life, and to her faith in a God present in the midst of it all. She refused to give in to the hatred that consumed many around her." Instead Etty wrote, "If I have one duty in these times, it is to bear witness. . . . We must be willing to act as a balm for all wounds."

- Do you know people either personally or through historical accounts who refused to let their anger turn into hatred? Are there those who can express anger without being consumed by it? Who express their gratitude for God's grace by living graciously, even when wronged?

- Can you think of times when you have been angry but you managed to treat the one who angered you as you would want to be treated by someone who was angry with you?

PRAYER

O God, you call us to treat others as we would wish them to treat us. How easy to forget this golden rule in the rush of anger! Give us the courage and the strength to love our neighbors as we love ourselves, at all times and in all places. Help us shape our anger for good rather than harm. Amen.

THE STORY

Read the story in Jonah 1:1–3; 3:1–5, 10; 4:1–4. Choose a way to experience the story from the "Bible Experience ideas" on page 23. As you read, try imagining that you are Jonah. Can you see things from his perspective?

> [1]Now the word of the Lord came to Jonah son of Amittai, saying, [2]"Go at once to Nineveh, that great city, and cry out against it; for their wickedness has come up before me." [3]But Jonah set out to flee to Tarshish from the presence of the Lord. He went down to Joppa and found a ship going to Tarshish; so he paid his fare and went on board, to go with them to Tarshish, away from the presence of the Lord.
> [3:1]The word of the Lord came to Jonah a second time, saying, [2]"Get up, go to Nineveh, that great city, and proclaim to it the message that I tell you." [3]So Jonah set out and went to Nineveh, according to the word of the Lord. Now Nineveh was an exceedingly large city, a three day's walk across. [4]Jonah began to go into the city, going a day's walk. And he

cried out, "Forty days more, and Nineveh will be overthrown!" ⁵And the people of Nineveh believed God; they proclaimed a fast, and everyone, great and small, put on sackcloth.

¹⁰When God saw what they did, how they turned from their evil ways, God changed his mind about the calamity that he had said he would bring upon them; and he did not do it.

⁴ˑ¹But this was very displeasing to Jonah, and he became angry. ²He prayed to the Lord and said, "O Lord! Is not this what I said while I was still in my own country? That is why I fled to Tarshish at the beginning; for I knew that you are a gracious God and merciful, slow to anger, and abounding in steadfast love, and ready to relent from punishing. ³And now, O Lord, please take my life from me, for it is better for me to die than to live." ⁴And the Lord said, "Is it right for you to be angry?"

YOU PUSH THE STORY

No matter where Jonah goes in this story—aboard a ship sailing to Tarshish, overboard into the sea, swallowed up by a great fish, or vomited (a fair translation of the descriptive Hebrew word used in the story) onto dry land—he cannot get away from God. In chapter 4 it becomes apparent that he cannot get away from his own anger either. What surprises you about this story? Review "The Story Behind the Story" on page 66 for more background information.

PUSH POSSIBILITIES FOR JONAH 3:1—4:11

- Why is Jonah so angry, from the beginning of the story until the end?
- What makes the Ninevites change their minds?
- Why is Jonah unhappy with the "success" of his own preaching?
- What was Jonah expecting God to do?
- Why does God hold back? What does it mean that God has a change of mind? What prevents Jonah from having a change of mind?

THE STORY PUSHES YOU

If you have ever feasted on anger, you have a taste of how Jonah felt when God told him to go to Nineveh as a prophet. Jonah was not confused about what God wanted him to do. Nor was Jonah afraid to go to Nineveh. It was not confusion or fear that propelled Jonah's abrupt flight in the opposite direction from Nineveh—it was self-righteous anger.

PUSH POSSIBILITIES

- Have you ever carried anger like Jonah's against others, whether individuals or groups of people? Do you feel that your anger was justified? Why or why not?

- Is anger ever healthy or called for? If you think so, when and why?

- What is judgment? What is mercy?

- When have you felt called to act mercifully towards someone who made you angry? What was the result?

THE STORY BEHIND THE STORY

Many prophets protest God's call—Moses said he couldn't speak clearly; Jeremiah said he was too young. But Jonah is downright disobedient. Why is Jonah so set against speaking God's call to repentance to Nineveh?

Nineveh was the capital city of Assyria; the Assyrians had conquered Israel in the eighth century BCE. The Assyrians were infamous for their cruelty to conquered peoples. Assyria was Israel's bitter enemy; Jonah was angry that God had ordered him to go to "these people," and he was angrier still to find that God would be compassionate toward those who had been so cruel. Jonah knew two things: that Nineveh was the enemy and that God was merciful. He didn't want to put the two together.

The book of Jonah might well be best read as a satire on the disobedience of Jonah and the persistence of God. The book is certainly unusual in the prophetic literature of the Hebrew Scriptures. First, Jonah is never actually named as a prophet. While his call is consistent with the call of other prophets, Jonah continues to refuse God's command even to the point of welcoming death. God, however, is not so easily thwarted and makes natural events conspire to ensure that Jonah goes where God requires him. Even when Jonah finally and grudgingly does obey, he delivers an almost parody of a prophetic message. Second, Jonah is sent to a city outside of Israel with which Israel had a particularly brutal history, as has been noted. Despite their vicious reputation and despite Jonah's mean-spirited sound bite of a message, the Ninevites do repent—so wholeheartedly that even their animals wear sackcloth and ashes.

There are many possible purposes to the book of Jonah, but clearly repentance is one message within the story. Repentance is available even to those like the Ninevites, who seem bent on ignoring God and living their own way. Repentance is also available to those who, like Jonah, run from God, are rude to God, and who choose to read events in the most negative way possible. Finally, repentance or turn-around is available even to God, who in the light of Ninevah's repentance decides not to carry out the promise to destroy the city.

 PUSH OUT

- Think of a situation or relationship that makes you angry. What is your best hope? Write out a short scenario that describes the transformation you wish to see happen. What do you say and do? How is that received? What do you learn about how you want to handle the situation? Do your feelings change? Are you able to see a first step that may move you toward what you hope to see happen?

- The movie of the play about Mozart in Vienna, *Amadeus* (Thorn EMI/HBO Video, 1984), is a great example of the sort of self-righteous anger Jonah displays. The character Salieri is consumed by anger at God for not participating in destroying Mozart, whom Salieri is jealous of and hates. Watch the movie with attention to the effects of anger.

- In various countries today, aboriginal peoples are demanding reconciliation from the nations that colonized their lands. Learn more about these efforts. Canada's Statement of Reconciliation with Aboriginal Peoples can be found at <www.usak.ca/nativelaw/newsletter.pdf>. For information about the United Church of Canada's involvement in reconciliation efforts, go to the United Church of Canada Current Resources: Justice and Reconciliation Web page at <www.uccan.org/resources/0886223776.htm>.

- The Australian organization, the Foundation for Aboriginal and Islander Research Action, can be found at <www.faira.org.au>. The Uniting Church in Australia is involved in reconciliation with aboriginal peoples. Learn more at the site for the Uniting Aboriginal and Islander Christian Congress at <http://nat.uca.org.au/au/uaicc>.

GROUP IDEAS   [Focus: To travel the line between judgment and mercy.

LIFE'S A PUSH

- Bring a picture or a toy of a whale as a focal point for the meeting area, since most people associate the story of Jonah with the whale.

- Read the two vignettes on pages 63–64 and talk about the issues raised in the questions provided.

- Pray together the prayer on page 64 or offer one of your own.

THE STORY

- Use the background material from "The Story Behind the Story" on pages 66–67 to introduce the group to the book of Jonah.

- Ask a volunteer to read the first chapter of the book of Jonah. How familiar is the group with the details of the story?

- Read chapter 2 as a litany—each person reading one verse of Jonah's psalm of thanksgiving. Discuss Jonah's prayer.

- Ask someone to read Jonah 3:1–4. What is the group's impression of how Jonah feels about being called a second time to go to Nineveh?

- Discuss Jonah's message to Nineveh. What impact does the group think Jonah anticipated his message would have on the city?

- Ask another person to read Jonah 3:5–10. How do group members react to the Ninevites' quick turn-around? to God's change of mind?

- Ask a fourth person to read Jonah 4:1–5. Discuss the exchange between Jonah and God.

- Have someone read Jonah 4:6–11. Take single words from group members to describe the relationship between Jonah and God.

YOU PUSH THE STORY

- Discuss how the story of Jonah portrays God.

- Discuss the push possibilities on page 65.

THE STORY PUSHES YOU

- Ask group members to look at the story on pages 64–65 as it relates to their own lives. Does Jonah in flight from God feel familiar? Do group members sometimes feel Jonah's reluctance to do what God asks? Has anyone in the group ever been angry—terribly angry—with God? Is the idea of God's compassionate grace towards all people a source of joy and comfort, or is it sometimes a challenge?

▪ Choose further items for discussion from the push possibilities on page 66.

Push Out

▪ Have the group talk about the ways they can turn from anger toward people and situations in the world to compassion for those people and those situations. What concrete ideas or strategies might the group decide to enlist in their spiritual journey around these issues—spiritual disciplines, community action, group study?

▪ Choose one or more of the push out ideas on page 67 to do together as a group, and plan for it.

▪ Allow time for the group to sit quietly. Ask them to imagine God's compassion and grace surrounding them. Imagine what it feels like to be held gently in that compassion, to be supported by it, to be healed by it. Then ask them to imagine God's compassion surrounding the whole world. Imagine how limitless, how powerful, how healing that compassion for the world can be. Close with a prayer asking God to send the group out to their homes, their communities, and their world surrounded by the power and strength of compassion and grace.

6. [GREAT INSPIRATIONS

Now there was a man in Jerusalem whose name was
Simeon; this man was righteous and devout, looking
forward to the consolation of Israel, and the Holy Spirit
rested on him. . . . Guided by the Spirit, Simeon came
into the temple; and when the parents brought in the
child Jesus, to do for him what was customary under the
law, Simeon took him in his arms and praised God.

Luke 2:25, 27–28

"If I hadn't believed it, I wouldn't have seen it for
myself." Recognizing God's presence in our lives
and in our world is part of the art and practice of
faith.

LIFE'S A PUSH

Howard Thurman was a well-known poet, mystic, philosopher, and theologian.
A much-beloved pastor, he had a deep and abiding spiritual life, and he guided
others with skill and grace. The following is a portion of one of his reflections,
"We Are Visited," from *The Centering Moment*:

It is our great and blessed fortune that our lives are never left to themselves alone. We are visited in ways that we can understand and in ways
that are beyond our understanding, by highlights, great moments of inspiration, quiet reassurances of grace, simple manifestations of gratuitous
expressions of the goodness of life. . . . We are also surrounded by the witness of those others whose strivings have made possible so much upon
which we draw from the common reservoir of our heritage, those who
have carried the light against the darkness, those who have persevered
when to persevere seemed idiotic and suicidal, those who have forgotten
themselves in the full and creative response to something that calls them
beyond the furthest reaches of their dreams and their hopes.

We are surrounded also by the witness of the life of the spirit in pecu-
liar ways that speak directly to our hearts and to our needs: those men and

women who walk the pages of the holy book; those men and women with whom in our moments of depression and despair, and in our moments of joy and delight, we identify.

We are grateful to Thee . . . for all of the springs of joy and renewal and recreation that are our common heritage and our common lot.[1]

- When have you felt visited with inspiration and grace?
- Who are the holy witnesses of God's love in your life?
- Identify some of the "springs of joy and renewal and recreation" in your experience of faith.

THE PARADOXICAL COMMANDMENTS

In 1968, a 19-year-old sophomore at Harvard College named Kent Keith wrote a booklet for high school student leaders called "The Silent Revolution: Dynamic Leadership in the Student Council." Keith included in the piece something he called "The Paradoxical Commandments." Amazingly, these "Paradoxical Commandments" have taken on a life of their own since then, and are still being sighted in various forms around the world. (Sightings are listed on the Web site <www.paradoxicalcommandments.com>.) Mother Teresa even had a version of them that had been reformatted into a poem hanging on the wall of her children's home in Calcutta, India. Kent Keith went on to become Dr. Kent M. Keith, the author of *Anyway: The Paradoxical Commandments: Finding Personal Meaning in a Crazy World* (New York: G. P. Putnam's Sons, 2002), and is a member of Monoa Valley United Church of Christ in Honolulu, Hawaii. Here are his "Paradoxical Commandments":

1. People are illogical, unreasonable, and self-centered.
   Love them anyway.

2. If you do good, people will accuse you of selfish ulterior motives.
   Do good anyway.

3. If you are successful, you win false friends and true enemies.
   Succeed anyway.

4. The good you do today will be forgotten tomorrow.
   Do good anyway.

5. Honesty and frankness make you vulnerable.
   Be honest and frank anyway.

6. The biggest men and women with the biggest ideas can be shot down by the smallest men and women with the smallest minds.
   Think big anyway.

7. People favor underdogs but follow only top dogs.
   Fight for a few underdogs anyway.

8. What you spend years building may be destroyed overnight.
   Build anyway.

9. People really need help but may attack you if you do help them.
   Help them anyway.

10. Give the world the best you have and you'll get kicked in the teeth.
    Give the world the best you have anyway.[2]

- Which of these "commandments" make you feel the least comfortable? which make the most sense to you? which inspire you?

- Who comes to mind when you read these? Is there someone you know who seems to live these out? Why do you think Mother Teresa posted a version of these in her children's home?

- What connections do you make between these and what you know about Jesus? about the church? about your own understanding of faith?

PRAYER

Reveal yourself to us, O God. Make us mindful of your presence.

Amen.

THE STORY

Read the story in Luke 2:21–38. Choose a way to experience the story from "Bible Experience ideas" on page 23. The celebrations and wonder of this story lend themselves to artistic expression.

> [21]After eight days had passed, it was time to circumcise the child; and he was called Jesus, the name given by the angel before he was conceived in the womb.
>
> [22]When the time came for their purification according to the law of Moses, they brought him up to Jerusalem to present him to the Lord [23](as it is written in the law of the Lord, "Every firstborn male shall be designated as holy to the Lord"), [24]and they offered a sacrifice according to what is stated in the law of the Lord, "a pair of turtledoves or two young pigeons."
>
> [25]Now there was a man in Jerusalem whose name was Simeon; this man was righteous and devout, looking forward to the consolation of Israel, and the Holy Spirit rested on him. [26]It had been revealed to him by the Holy Spirit that he would not see death before he had seen the

Lord's Messiah. [27]Guided by the Spirit, Simeon came into the temple; and when the parents brought in the child Jesus, to do for him what was customary under the law, [28]Simeon took him in his arms and praised God, saying,

[29]"Master, now you are dismissing your servant in peace,
according to your word;
[30]for my eyes have seen your salvation,
[31]which you have prepared in the presence of all peoples,
[32]a light for revelation to the Gentiles
and for glory to your people Israel."

[33]And the child's father and mother were amazed at what was being said about him. [34]Then Simeon blessed them and said to his mother Mary, "This child is destined for the falling and the rising of many in Israel, and to be a sign that will be opposed [35]so that the inner thoughts of many will be revealed—and a sword will pierce your own soul too."
[36]There was also a prophet, Anna the daughter of Phanuel, of the tribe of Asher. She was of a great age, having lived with her husband seven years after her marriage, [37]then as a widow to the age of eighty-four. She never left the temple but worshiped there with fasting and prayer night and day. [38]At that moment she came, and began to praise God and to speak about the child to all who were looking for the redemption of Jerusalem.

YOU PUSH THE STORY

What is intriguing about this story? What do you want to know more about—the rituals, the characters, or the setting? Push this account of an early revelation of the identity of Jesus with your questions, frustrations, doubts, and curiosity.

PUSH POSSIBILITIES FOR LUKE 2:21–38

- Mary and Joseph are portrayed as faithfully adhering to the practices of their religion. Imagine how growing up in this family would have shaped Jesus. Why do you think it's important for Luke to include these details?

- Who are Simeon and Anna and how did they recognize Jesus?

- What does "the consolation of Israel" mean and why would Jesus be identified with it?

- What is Simeon saying that Jesus will be and do?

- What did Simeon mean when he said that a sword would pierce Mary's soul also?

- What would Anna have said to the people "who were looking for the redemption of Jerusalem?"

HE STORY PUSHES YOU

How does this story push you to examine your own spiritual life? to recognize the presence of Christ in the world?

PUSH POSSIBILITIES FOR LUKE 2:21–38

- Do you know people who, like Simeon, could be described as having the Holy Spirit rest on them? Do you know people who, like Anna, worship God with power, strength, and devotion? Do you know people who have waited a long time for the promises they believe they have received from God to be fulfilled?

- What do the examples of Mary and Joseph and Simeon and Anna have to say to us about our spiritual disciplines, our practice of prayer, and the ways in which we seek a relationship with God? What does it mean to slow down, to take time, to focus, and to simplify so that we can recognize God's presence day to day?

- How would you compare the faithful persistence of Anna and Simeon with people who work their whole lives for social-justice transformation, based on their commitment to and belief in God's realm on earth?

THE STORY BEHIND THE STORY

It is very important that readers of Luke's Gospel understand Jesus to be both the one promised by God who would come to save Israel and a pious Israelite who understood and observed all of the traditions and teachings of the law. Jesus was circumcised eight days after his birth, an act that marked male children as both dedicated to God and as members of the covenant community (see Genesis 17:9–14). Following circumcision, two further acts were required. As a reminder of God's action in the Exodus, all firstborn males were redeemed by first being dedicated to God and then being bought back by their parents at the price of five shekels of silver (see Numbers 18:15–16). This was followed by rites of purification. After the birth of a male child, a mother was considered ritually unclean for seven days and was required to undergo baths of purification for thirty-three days during which time she was forbidden to enter the temple. After a period of forty days (if the child was female the time period was doubled), the mother was required to offer a sacrifice at the temple of a lamb and a pigeon. If the family could not afford a lamb and a pigeon, two pigeons would suffice (which is what we read that Mary and Joseph were able to bring).

The temple was the center of Jewish religious life. It is here that Jesus is brought by his devout parents, and it is here at the symbolic heart of God's interaction with Israel that Jesus is recognized by a pious man and a prophetic woman. Both Anna and Simeon are portrayed as archetypal faithful Israelites: Anna, as a prophet and widow in the tradition of Miriam, Deborah, and Judith; and Simeon, as a faithful man waiting and looking for God to deliver God's people. Simeon's blessing and desire for the "consolation" of Israel echoes the book of Isaiah, where the prophet promises that God will comfort God's people (Isaiah 40:1–2; 51:3; 52:9). It was only when all that was required by the law was done that Jesus and his parents returned home.

PUSH OUT

The focus on practices of faith in this session invites us to consider how we might seek transformation for ourselves and our world through intentional spirituality. As you explore and experience these push out ideas, what do you notice about the interplay between expressing spirituality through worship or prayer and through action? If you are more inclined to choose either action or contemplation in preference to the other, push yourself in new directions. How might each enrich the other?

- How would a Simeon or an Anna recognize the presence of Christ in you or your faith community? Take a close look at ways in which your church or denomination reaches out to the broader community. How are you involved?

- What difference might it make in your life if you practiced prayer and worship more intentionally? If you asked God to open not just your eyes but also your heart to the world, in what ways might you be given more glimpses of God's revelation and salvation? How might "seeing with the heart" change your relationships with others? relationships within your group or church? relationships among people and countries in the world? Choose a particular relationship or circumstance and make a practice of praying or meditating about that situation for at least one month. How do you change? How do things change?

- Dr. Howard Thurman founded the first interracial interdenominational church in the United States—the Church for the Fellowship of All Peoples, in San Francisco. He was dean of the Chapel at Boston

University. Born in a segregated Florida town in 1900, he was at the time of his death in 1981 recognized as one of the century's foremost religious leaders. To read a thorough yet succinct biography of Thurman, go to <www.africanpubs.com/Apps/bios/1090ThurmanHoward.asp?pic=none>. *With Head and Heart: The Autobiography of Howard Thurman* (New York: Harcourt Brace Jovanovich, 1979) is the excellent and inspiring story of this deeply spiritual Christian leader.

- Read Thomas Merton's classic on the nature of prayer, *Contemplative Prayer* (New York: Image Books, 1971).

- "My spirit within me keeps vigil for you. My soul yearns for you in the night." The monastic office in the Roman Catholic tradition includes an "Hour of Vigils" that is prayed during the night while it is still dark in the hours before dawn. Praying these prayers in the dark is a way of symbolizing the spirit of everyone who waits for God. The office is prayed with all those who long and yearn for the coming of Christ into the world.

  The Benedictine nuns at the Jamberoo Abbey in New South Wales, Australia, observe the Hour of Vigils at 4:30 in the morning. The daily celebration of the Hour of Vigils, these sisters say, makes Christians more aware "that Christ is coming at every moment, in every person, in every situation." The coming of the dawn in the hours that follow the Hour of Vigils is symbolic of the coming of Christ's light into the world. The Hour of Vigils reminds us that, as Christians, we must always be on the watch, prepared for Christ's coming.

  Pray the sentences quoted above from the Hour of Vigils, remembering in your prayers the people and places in the world that need Christ's presence so desperately. You might even consider praying this prayer before dawn for a week or once a week for a month. What fresh insights come to you in these early morning hours and as the light breaks through to a new day?

- Get information on programs such as Doctors without Borders, a private, non-profit organization that delivers emergency aid to victims of armed conflict, epidemics, and natural disasters at <www.doctorswithoutborders.org> or The Befriending Network, a British organization that provides help to caregivers of the handicapped and the terminally ill at <www.befriending.co.uk>.Go to a Web site for peace work at <www.pax.protest.net> for a list of vigils, meetings, and teach-ins around the world and in your own community. Imagine the consolation these groups bring to others. How can you get involved?

- Commit to getting involved—through prayer and action—with some group or organization that tries to see the world with the heart as well as with the eyes. The Global Ideas Bank at <www.globalideasbank.org> has links to many ideas and organizations at work in the world. As you get involved with some group or activity, share ways you see God's revelation breaking into the world.

 **GROUP IDEAS**

[Focus: To explore ways to attune ourselves more fully to God's presence and work in the world.

LIFE'S A PUSH

■ Post pictures of people at prayer in various places and in various ways. Collect pictures of sacred places where people pray. Bring icons of saints or photos of spiritual leaders and place these on the floor in the center of the room, with chairs set up in a circle. Place a lighted candle on a small table in the center of the room or on the floor. Have small individual candles available, one for each group member.

■ Introduce Howard Thurman to the group with the information from Push Out on pages 75–76 and have everyone read "We Are Visited" on pages 70–71. Discuss the questions on page 71.

■ Invite a volunteer to read "The Paradoxical Commandments" on pages 71–72.

■ Pray the prayer on page 72 or one of your own.

THE STORY

■ Invite the group to read the background material from "The Story Behind the Story" on pages 74–75 before reading the story.

■ Ask for volunteers to read the parts of narrator and Simeon from the story on pages 72–73. Invite the rest of the group to imagine that they are bystanders at the temple that day, seeing Simeon and Anna's responses to the baby.

■ Discuss the experience of the bystanders. Were any of them skeptical? hopeful but dubious? Did anyone understand the importance of what was being proclaimed?

YOU PUSH THE STORY

■ Talk in general terms about how people respond to prophecies and proclamations of God's intentions. Is it difficult for people to believe good news of hope in a world of disappointment and disillusionment?

■ Discuss the push possibilities on pages 73–74.

THE STORY PUSHES YOU

■ Invite participants to spend a few minutes writing their responses to one or more of the push possibilities on page 74. Allow time for those who are comfortable doing so to share their responses.

PUSH OUT

- Create and commit to a new discipline of prayer as a group. This might be journaling, weekly prayer meetings, or reading the newspaper and praying about specific events and for people in the news. Decide how long you will keep the discipline as a group and choose a time and place to talk about the experience.

- Choose a push out from pages 75–76 to do together as a group and plan for it.

- If you have small individual candles, invite each member to light one from a candle in the center of the group as they sit in a circle. As they light each candle, have them pray silently for God's help in their efforts to see the world with the heart.

1. Howard Thurman, *The Centering Moment* (Richmond, Ind.: Friends United Press, 1980), 54. Used by permission.
2. Kent M. Keith, "The Paradoxical Commandments," © Copyright Kent M. Keith 1968, 2001, <www.paradoxicalcommandments.com>, *Anyway: The Paradoxical Commandments*, G. P. Putnam's Sons, 2002. Used by permission.

7. [MORE THAN BUMPER STICKERS

For God so loved the world that God gave God's only Child, that whoever believes in that child should not perish but have eternal life.[1]

John 3:16

There is a tension in the life of faith between making claims about what we believe and staying open to the mystery of all that we cannot know about God. It's hard to put mystery on a bumper sticker!

LIFE'S A PUSH

LOOKING FOR THE WORDS

It can be downright frustrating trying to talk to people about what you believe. You can say one word that has all kinds of meanings, and no matter how much you try to "unpack" it, people can interpret what you say in ways that have nothing to do with what you believe. Words like "salvation," or "born again," or "eternal life" can flood us with feelings and assumptions that make it hard to listen to one another. Sometimes misinterpretation can lead to disrespect, discounting of one another, and even dangerous conflicts.

Look over the following religious quotations and catchphrases. Which ones intrigue you and even help you express your faith?

What Would Jesus Do?

Where your treasure is, there will your heart be also. (Jesus)

Jesus is my copilot.

In prayer one should always unite herself or himself with the community. (The Talmud)

God said it. I believe it. That settles it.

God don't make no junk.

Through selfless service, you will always be fruitful and find fulfillment. (Bhagavad Gita)

I am God. Today I will be handling all of your problems. Please remember that I do not need your help. If life happens to deliver a situation to you that you cannot handle, do not attempt to resolve it. Kindly put it in the SFGTD (Something for God to do) box.

- What other responses did you have to these quotations? Are there any that turn you off or annoy you? Are there others that come to mind?
- Take a moment and compose your own bumper sticker or short quote that says something about your faith.

Consider this experience of Jim Reilly, staff reporter at *The Post-Standard* in Syracuse, New York:

> I recently read a newspaper article about two men in my community, Michael and Nick. They have been caring for AIDS patients in their home for the past nine years, without charging anything. When asked why they do what they do, they point to the ways Jesus showed compassion to the stranger, especially the poor, the sick, and the rejected. But they admit they would rather live their faith than talk about it. "There's so much crap that's talked about when people talk about faith. It makes it hard even to use the language," Nick says.[2]

- Think of someone you know who expresses their faith without saying a thing. What do you know about what they believe from what they do?
- Compare the version of John 3:16 at the beginning of this session with the New Revised Standard Version or other version from a Bible you have. Reflect on the differences. What do they mean to you?

MISSING EACH OTHER

For a couple of years I worked with a group from our church in an after-school program at a public housing community center. One day when we were wrapping up our part of the program, a pastor of a nearby church approached me from across the parking lot. He was coming to lead the children's weekly Bible study. The pastor planted his feet squarely in front of me and asked what I was doing at the center and asked if I was helping to teach the children about salvation. I told him that we invite the children to church and that we hoped we helped build their self-esteem, build their trust, and encourage them to express their feelings in healthy ways. I said I thought we were teaching about salvation without using those words. He looked me in the eye and told me all that stuff is not the gospel and told me that unless I changed my ways, he'd have to tell the kids at the center that I was doing the devil's work. He turned, got into his van, and drove away. Though we both professed to be Christian, our words were completely missing each other. And it hurt.

- Why do you think this was a painful encounter?
- Have you ever experienced being misunderstood when you were trying to describe your beliefs? How did you feel? How did you respond?

PRAYER

Some religious traditions believe that our intentional time with God is best spent in silence, shedding words and thoughts and simply letting the presence of God wash over us. Sit in the quiet for five minutes and focus awareness on your breathing and on the air passing in through your nostrils or mouth. Don't interfere with your breathing; just observe it. As thoughts come to you, try to imagine them as air bubbles rising to the surface of a pond and breaking. Then simply refocus on your breath.

A man, a religious leader, comes to Jesus at night. They engage in something of a language dance. Jesus will not be pinned down to narrow explanations or easy answers about the way God works in the world.

THE STORY

Read the Bible story from the Gospel of John. Then choose one or more ways to experience it from the suggestions on pages 17–23. This is a good story in which to focus on specific words that can have more than one meaning, creating poetry, or artwork, or creative-writing pieces. Use "The Story Behind the Story" on pages 83–84 as a reference.

[1]Now there was a Pharisee named Nicodemus, a leader of the Jews. [2]He came to Jesus by night and said to him, "Rabbi, we know that you are a teacher who has come from God; for no one can do these signs that you do apart from the presence of God." [3]Jesus answered him, "Very truly, I tell you, no one can see the kingdom of God without being born from above." [4]Nicodemus said to him, "How can anyone be born after having grown old? Can one enter a second time into the mother's womb and be born?" [5]Jesus answered, "Very truly, I tell you, no one can enter the kingdom of God without being born of water and Spirit. [6]What is born

of the flesh is flesh, and what is born of the Spirit is spirit. [7]Do not be astonished that I said to you, 'You must be born from above.' [8]The wind blows where it chooses, and you hear the sound of it, but you do not know where it comes from or where it goes. So it is with everyone who is born of the Spirit." [9]Nicodemus said to him, "How can these things be?" [10]Jesus answered him, "Are you a teacher of Israel, and yet you do not understand these things?

[11]"Very truly, I tell you, we speak of what we know and testify to what we have seen; yet you do not receive our testimony. [12]If I have told you about earthly things and you do not believe, how can you believe if I tell you about heavenly things? [13]No one has ascended into heaven except the one who descended from heaven, the Son of Man. [14]And just as Moses lifted up the serpent in the wilderness, so must the Son of Man be lifted up, [15]that whoever believes in him may have eternal life."

[16]"For God so loved the world that he gave his only Son, so that everyone who believes in him may not perish but may have eternal life."

[17]"Indeed, God did not send the Son into the world to condemn the world, but in order that the world might be saved through him."

YOU PUSH THE STORY

There are lots of nuances and double-meanings in this exchange between two religious leaders. Push the story with your questions. What is confusing? What makes you curious?

PUSH POSSIBILITIES FOR JOHN 3:1–17

- From the story, what does "born again" seem to mean for Jesus?
- Why does Nicodemus call Jesus "Rabbi"?
- What clues about "eternal life" does the story give?
- Who is the Son of Man?
- What do "spirit" and "flesh" mean in the story?
- What is the "lifting up a serpent" part about?
- Why does Nicodemus come in darkness? What or whom does Nicodemus represent?

THE STORY PUSHES YOU

How does the story provoke you? What does it call out in our spiritual lives?

PUSH POSSIBILITIES FOR JOHN 3:1–17

- Does this story invite us to make a decision; to take a stand?
- What does the story say about staying in dialogue even when someone doesn't get where you're coming from?
- As a metaphor for salvation, what does the notion of being born again help you think about?
- What are the different ways to think about eternal life? Is salvation just about what happens when we die or does it impact our hope for today?
- How does the story help us to think about interfaith dialogue, relationships, and collaboration?
- What is your current understanding of what Jesus says in this passage?

THE STORY BEHIND THE STORY

The writer of John wrote this Gospel to a faction of the Jewish community that believed Jesus was the Messiah. Due to their beliefs, they were expelled from the synagogue and were experiencing difficult times as a persecuted religious minority. The writer uses lots of figures of speech in order to avoid over-simple representations but also to challenge the reader into making a decision to follow Jesus. The story was written probably two generations after the time Jesus lived, during a time of religious turmoil.

Nicodemus comes to Jesus calling him, "Rabbi" or teacher. Yet he speaks on behalf of his religious community. He says "We know," but his knowledge also brings with it certain assumptions. Jesus can't help but challenge some of Nicodemus's assumptions. He plays with Nicodemus's language to help him see that "we know" is not altogether true.

The author draws on the Jewish wisdom tradition in portraying Jesus as one who plays with words, using lots of language and images of the Hebrew Scriptures. Nicodemus first gets confused when Jesus talks about being born "from above." The Greek word used in the story has a double meaning. *Anothen* can mean both born from above or born again or born anew. Nicodemus understands only one of its meanings and asks how any grown person can go back into a mother's womb. Jesus plays with this understanding by talking of being born "of water and Spirit." Jesus talks about a birth breaking the water of a womb as well as a spiritual birth—a birth into the Kingdom of God.

Jesus continues the playful words in talking about the Spirit. The Greek word *pneuma* he uses also has two meanings. It can mean "wind" as well as "spirit." It is a mystery beyond human knowledge or control. It's like the wind. You don't know where it comes from or where it goes, but you know it's here. Jesus, upon his death in John's story, sends the community the Spirit, who hosts, comforts, and helps make it possible to come to know God through the One who is lifted up on the cross.

Then Jesus lays on one more wordplay when he says that the Son of Man will be lifted up, just as Moses lifted up the serpent in the wilderness. In Numbers 21:8–9 of the Hebrew Scripture, Moses takes a poisonous serpent and puts it on a pole. Anyone who is bitten by a snake in the plague of snakes sent by God could look at the serpent on the pole and live. Those who know that the Son of Man is lifted up live with God. They see the danger and judgment and can decide to know life with God. The word for "lifted up" also means "exalted." The gospel writer understands that Jesus will be lifted up on the cross and be raised from the dead and ascend to God, all in one continuous motion of being "exalted."

The rest of the Gospel of John gives us some help in understanding eternal life, not as something reserved for time after death but as an unending relationship with God. Through the rest of the Gospel of John we read of Jesus who is bread and drink that will not leave us hungry or thirsty (4:13–15, 6:35), a true vine that bears the fruit of love (15:1–11), and a comforter sent to teach us and help us remember, even after Jesus' death (14:25–27). Eternal life describes a change in human existence brought about by Jesus. Jesus' questions to Nicodemus become questions to us. Jesus in John is asking us to make a decision to be born into a new way of being in the world, not just as individuals being converted by what we do or believe but as persons willing to receive the counsel of the Spirit in a community who "knows."

PUSH OUT

Consider some of the following push outs as ways to more deeply engage the complexity of the passage.

- Consider participating in dialogue circles with persons of other faiths, not so much to talk about the content of faith (doctrines and dogma) but to share how faith gets lived out in daily decisions, family and community rituals, and everyday ways of being and doing. Ask people to bring their own refreshments to share (in order to be sensitive to dietary practices) and questions to help get the conversation going. Invite people to share stories. The National Conference for Community and Justice has some helpful resources in the area of interfaith dialogue. Their Web site is <www.nccj.org>.

- Look for ways that movies, TV shows, and the news portray religions in ways that oversimplify their complex systems of belief. Engage in public-awareness campaigns in your local community that address these stereotypes. Declare your faith community or study circle an "Intolerance Free Zone" and discuss what that means in the ways you structure your life together.

- Create a kite, windsock, or flag to catch the wind and show its presence. Decorate it with words or images that express the ways you would like to be born anew into the richness and joy of life with God.

- Spend some time in silent prayer. Anthony de Mello's book, *Sadhana, a Way to God: Christian Exercises in Eastern Form* (Liguori, Mo.: Liguori/Triumph, 1998), offers lots of exercises in this form of prayer.

- "*An Inclusive Language Lectionary* is a major attempt to recast the language of scripture so that it addresses women and men equally. The church has never believed that God is male or that God speaks to the church in male-oriented language more relevant to men than to women."[3] Research your denomination's position on inclusive language. What is your position on it?

ROUP IDEAS

Focus: To explore, express, and celebrate the complexity of faith.

LIFE'S A PUSH

- Provide strips of plain paper that are about the size of a typical bumper sticker and markers, enough for everyone in the group.

- Invite volunteers to read the scenarios provided in the session on pages 80–81.

- Discuss selected questions on pages 80–81.

- Have participants create their own faith bumper stickers and share them with the group.

- Lead the time of silent prayer as described on page 81.

THE STORY

- Have participants read the story on pages 80–81 to themselves. Then invite three people to read aloud the parts of the narrator, Jesus, and Nicodemus.

- Choose a method of experiencing the story from page 23. Opportunities that really delve into the meaning of words and phrases of the story are important for this session.

YOU PUSH THE STORY

- List on newsprint ways that the story comforts and challenges the participants, and list any questions or doubts that emerge. Explore "The Story Behind the Story" on pages 83–84 for information that may address some of these.

- Work through the push possibilities on page 82 together.

THE STORY PUSHES YOU

- Invite participants to close their eyes. Read one of the pushes on page 83 and ask them to meditate on it for a few moments.

- Open up the discussion by rereading the question and asking people to open their eyes and share their responses.

- Discuss the other story pushes.

PUSH OUT

- Identify as a group one of the push outs on page 85 you would like to do and engage in planning for the experience.

- Create group guidelines for conversation that will help keep dialogue open and allow everyone to feel comfortable about making their contributions to discussions. Make the list into a poster and display it, referring to it in future sessions.

- Offer the prayer below or one of your own.

PRAYER

May our words here, O God, add meaning to the ways you work in our lives. May our words here, O God, become your living word. Send us forth to worship and serve you in word and deed. Amen.

1. *An Inclusive Language Lectionary: Readings for Year B, rev. ed.* (Atlanta, Ga.: John Knox Press; New York: The Pilgrim Press; Philadelphia: The Westminister Press, 1987), 240.
2. Jim Reilly, "We Need Time to Grieve," *The Post-Standard*, November 4, 2001, sec. 1, 1–2.
3. *An Inclusive Language Lectionary*, 7.

8. [UP A TREE

Jesus came and said to him, "Zacchaeus, hurry and come down; for I must stay at your house today."
Luke 19:5

The presence of Jesus makes room for the rejected to be accepted, the lost to be found, and the foolish to be wise.

IFE'S A PUSH

SURPRISING WISDOM

Sometimes it takes being up-ended a bit or being humbled to experience a transformation. Other times connecting with the child within opens up possibilities for change and growth.

Once when I was working through the church with young adults with Down's syndrome, a man named Peter became quite fond of me. We often did art projects together. One day Peter asked if the two of us could go for a walk in the village center near the church. We walked, arm in arm. Peter stopped often and wept, burying his head in my shoulder. I felt a bit uncertain about what to do, how to be supportive. Actually I found the whole thing downright awkward. When we got to the fountain in the center of the village, we stood and watched the many people doing their errands, working in the shops, sweeping the street, and parking their cars. In the center of all this activity, Peter threw his arms around me and held me tightly. He then proclaimed with all the volume his lungs could muster, "I love you! I love you!" I was startled and embarrassed. It was the first time I could remember someone not part of my family showing so much public affection for me. But Peter knew exactly what he was doing. He broke through my cautious awkwardness. He became my host and teacher on future walks to the center of the village. Peter helped me see how showing feelings could bring joy. He helped me to see how affection and appropriate touch are not things to be feared but are often wonderful ways to deepen friendship.

THE CANTOR AND THE KLANSMAN

Hatred and bitterness can never cure the disease of fear; only love can do that. Hatred paralyzes life; love releases it. Hatred confuses life. Love harmonizes it. Hatred darkens life; love illuminates it.

—Martin Luther King Jr.

One sunny Sunday morning in June 1991, Cantor Michael Weisser and his wife, Julie, surrounded by half unpacked boxes in the kitchen of their new home in Lincoln, Nebraska, were talking and laughing with a friend when the phone rang.

Michael, who answered with his usual warmth, heard a harsh and hateful voice say slowly and loudly: "You will be sorry you ever moved in [to that house], Jew boy!" Then the line went dead.

Two days later, the Weissers received a thick brown packet in the mail with a card on top that read, "The KKK is watching you, Scum." The stack of flyers and brochures included ugly caricatures of Jews, blacks, and "Race Traitors" being shot and hung and spelled out other threatening messages, including, "Your time is up!" and "The Holohoax was nothing compared to what's going to happen to you."

The Weissers called the police, who said the hate mail looked like the work of Larry Trapp, who was the state leader, known as the "Grand Dragon" of the Ku Klux Klan. Also an avowed Nazi, Trapp was suspected of leading skinheads and Klansmen who had been terrorizing black, Vietnamese and Jewish families in Nebraska and Iowa.

"He's dangerous," the police warned. "We know he makes explosives." They advised the Weissers to keep the doors locked and call if they received any unlabeled packages—just in case Trapp sent a letter bomb.

Although Trapp, forty-four, was diabetic and in a wheelchair, he was a major Midwestern link in the national white supremacist movement. He was, in fact, responsible for the fire-bombings of several African-Americans' homes around Lincoln and for what he called "Operation Gooks," the burning of the Indo-Chinese Refugee Assistance Center in Omaha. At the time, he was making plans to bomb B'nai Jeshurun, the synagogue where Weisser was the spiritual leader.

Trapp lived alone on the southwest side of Lincoln in a cramped one-room apartment. On one wall he kept a giant Nazi flag and a double-life-size picture of Hitler. Next to these hung his white cotton Klan robe with its red belt and hood. He kept an arsenal of assault rifles, pistols and shotguns within reach in case his perceived "enemies" came crashing through his door.

After the hate mail, Julie Weisser began to wonder about Trapp, who had gone public to recruit new members of the Klan. She was struck by how lonely he must be, how isolated in all his hatred. She found out where he lived and sometimes would drive past his apartment complex. While she felt infuriated and revolted by him, she was also intrigued by how he could become so evil. She told Michael she had an idea. She was going to send Trapp a letter every day, along with a passage from Proverbs–her favorite book of the Bible–one that talks about how to treat your fellow man and conduct your life.

Michael liked the idea, but didn't want Julie to sign her name. And friends were horrified, warning that Trapp was crazy and violent and might try to kill her.

"He's the one who does things anonymously," Julie responded. "I won't do that." She held off on her plan, but later on, when Trapp launched a white supremacist series on a local-access cable channel, Michael Weisser was incensed. He called the number for the hotline of the KKK–"The Vigilante Voices of Nebraska"—and listened to Trapp's harsh voice spewing out a racist diatribe on the answering machine.

Michael called several times just to keep the line busy, but then began to leave his own messages. "Larry," he said, "Why do you hate me? You don't even know me, so how can you hate me?"

Anther time he said. "Larry, do you know that the first laws Hitler's Nazis passed were against people like yourself who had physical deformities, physical handicaps? Do you realize you would have been among the first to die under Hitler? Why do you love the Nazis so much?"

Whenever he thought of it, Michael called and left another message. One night, however, he asked Julie, "What will I do if the guy ever picks up the phone?"

"Tell him you want to do something nice for him." she said "Tell him you'll take him to the grocery store or something. Anything to help him. It will catch him totally off guard."

For weeks, Michael listened to Trapp's taped invectives denouncing "niggers," "queers," "kikes," and "gooks." Each time Weisser would reply with a message of his own. One day, just after Michael said, "Larry, when you give up hating, a world of love is waiting for you," Trapp, who was feeling increasingly annoyed by the calls, picked up the phone and shouted, "What the —— do you want?"

"I just want to talk to you," said Michael.

"Why the —— are you harassing me? Stop harassing me!"

"I don't want to harass you, Larry," Michael said. "I just want to talk to you."

"I know your voice. You black by any chance?"

"No, I'm Jewish."

"You are harassing me," said Trapp. "What do you want? Make it quick."

Michael remembered Julie's advice. "Well, I was thinking you might need a hand with something, and I wondered if I could help," he said. "I know you're in a wheelchair and I thought maybe I could take you to the grocery store or something."

Trapp couldn't think of anything to say. Michael listened to the silence. Finally, Trapp cleared his throat and, when he spoke, his voice sounded different.

"That's okay," he said. "That's nice of you, but I've got that covered. Thanks anyway. But don't call this number anymore."

Before Trapp could hang up, Michael replied, "I'll be in touch."

Michael's calls were making Trapp feel confused. And a letter he received from a former nurse in Lincoln also affected him. If you give your love to God "like you gave yourself to the KKK," she wrote, "he'll heal you of all that bitterness, hatred and hurt . . . in ways you won't believe."

Then, at a visit to his eye doctor, Trapp felt his wheelchair moving. "I helping you on elevator," said a young female voice behind him. He asked where she was from. "I from Vietnam," she said. That evening, he found himself crying as he thought about the scent of the woman's gardenia perfume, his memories of "Operation Gooks" and his assault on the Vietnamese community.

"I'm rethinking a few things," he told Michael in a subsequent phone call. But a few days later he was on TV, shrieking about "kikes" and "half-breeds" and "the Jews' media."

Furious, Michael called Trapp, who answered his phone. "It's clear you're not rethinking anything at all," Michael said, demanding an explanation.

In a tremulous voice, Trapp said, "I'm sorry I did that. I've been talking like that all of my life . . . I can't help it. . . . I'll apologize."

That evening, Michael Weisser asked his congregation to include in their prayers someone "who is sick from the illness of bigotry and hatred. Pray that he can be healed, too." Across town, Lenore Letcher, an African American woman whom Trapp had terrorized, also prayed for Trapp, "Dear God, let him find you in his heart."

That same night, the swastika rings Trapp wore on both hands began to sting and itch so much that he pulled them off—something he had never done before. All night, he tossed in his bed, restless, confused, and unsettled.

Around dinnertime the next day, the Weissers' phone rang. "I want to get out," Trapp said, "but I don't know how."

Michael suggested that he and Julie go over to Trapp's apartment to talk in person and "break bread together." Trapp hesitated, then finally agreed.

As they were preparing to leave, Julie started turning around, looking for a gift, and decided on a silver friendship ring of intertwined strands that Michael never wore.

"Good choice." said Michael. "I've always thought all those strands could represent all the different kinds of people on this earth." To Julie it was a symbol of how "somebody's life can be all twisted up and become very beautiful."

When the door to Trapp's apartment creaked open, Michael and Julie saw the bearded Larry Trapp in his wheelchair. An automatic weapon was slung over the doorknob and a Nazi flag hung on the wall. Michael took Trapp's hand, and Trapp winced as if hit by a jolt of electricity. Then he broke into tears.

He looked down at his two silver swastika rings. "Here, he said, yanking them off his fingers and putting them in Michael's hand. "I can't wear these anymore. Will you take them away?"

Michael and Julie looked at each other in stunned silence.

"Larry, we brought you a ring, too," Julie said, kneeling beside him and sliding the ring onto his finger. Larry began to sob. "I'm sorry for all the things I've done," he said. Michael and Julie put their arms around Larry and hugged him. Overwhelmed by emotion, they started crying, too.

On November 16, 1991, Trapp resigned from the Klan and soon quit all his racist organizations. Later, he wrote apologies to the many people he had threatened or abused. "I wasted the first forty years of my life and caused harm to other people," Larry said. "Now, I've learned we're one race and one race only."

On New Year's Eve, Trapp learned he had less that a year to live. That night, the Weissers invited him to move into their home, and he did so. They converted their living room into his bedroom. As his health deteriorated, Julie quit her job to take care of him. She fed him, waited on him, sometimes all through the night, emptying pans of vomit.

Having a remorseful, dying Klansman in their home was disruptive to the whole family, which included three teenagers, a dog and a cat, but everyone pitched in. Once Trapp said to Julie, "You and Michael are doing for me what my parents should have done. You're taking care of me."

On days when Larry was well enough, he listened to speeches by the Rev. Dr. Martin Luther King, Jr. and books on Gandhi and Malcolm X. He also began to listen to books on Judaism and to study the faith in earnest.

On June 25, 1992, Larry Trapp converted to Judaism in ceremonies at B'nai, Jeshurun, the very synagogue that he previously had planned to blow up. Three months later on September 6, 1992, he died in the Weisser home, with Michael and Julie beside him, holding his hands.

At Larry's funeral, Michael Weisser said, "Those of us who remain behind ask the questions. 'O Lord, what is man [sic]" We are like a breath, like a shadow that passes away . . .' And yet, somehow, we know there is more to our lives than what first meets the eye.[1]

- What do you think Trapp's removing the swastika rings symbolized for him?
- Has anyone in your life believed you could do something, even when you thought you couldn't? What did they do that gave you motivation to try?
- Have you ever experienced an immersion in someone else's experience and worldview that helped you to see something in yourself that is hard to look at? If so, what was that like? How might God be at work in those times?

PRAYER

Holy Healer, gift us with curiosity and persistence so that we might follow our hearts and discover new possibilities. Help us to let go of everything that blocks us from opening up to you. Amen.

Zacchaeus is a biblical character who truly follows his heart despite some real social pressure to "behave." His risk pays off in the form of acceptance and a chance to change his life.

THE STORY

Read the story from Luke 19:1–10 and then choose one or more ways to get into the story. Select from the Bible Experience ideas on page 23, according to what you think will help you explore this particular story most effectively.

¹He entered Jericho and was passing through it. ²A man was there named Zacchaeus; he was a chief tax collector and was rich. ³He was trying to see who Jesus was, but on account of the crowd he could not, because he was short in stature. ⁴So he ran ahead and climbed a sycamore tree to see him, because he was going to pass that way. ⁵When Jesus came to the place, he looked up and said to him, "Zacchaeus, hurry and come down; for I must stay at your house today." ⁶So he hurried down and was happy to welcome him. ⁷All who saw it began to grumble and said, "He has gone to be the guest of one who is a sinner." ⁸Zacchaeus stood there and said to the Lord, "Look, half of my possessions, Lord, I will give to the poor; and if I have defrauded anyone of anything, I will pay back four times as much." ⁹Then Jesus said to him, "Today salvation has come to this house, because he too is a son of Abraham. ¹⁰For the Son of Man came to seek out and to save the lost."

YOU PUSH THE STORY

Push this story of a tax collector, the crowd, and Jesus with questions, doubts, and curiosities. What is intriguing about this story? What makes you confused or frustrated? Here are a few push questions to get you started. Also use "The Story Behind the Story" on pages 95–96 to explore the story further.

PUSH POSSIBILITIES FOR LUKE 19:1–10

- Who is a chief tax collector and why is he despised?
- Why is Jesus so intent on staying at Zacchaeus's house?
- Why do people in the crowd react so strongly when Jesus invites himself to stay with Zacchaeus?
- What is the significance of the sycamore tree?
- Why is Zacchaeus so eager to see Jesus?
- What makes Zacchaeus suddenly say that he's going to start giving back what he has taken from people?
- What is the salvation that comes to Zacchaeus's house?

THE STORY PUSHES YOU

Allow the story to push back at your perceptions and way of life. What new perspectives is God inviting you into with this story?

PUSH POSSIBILITIES FOR LUKE 19:1–10

- What does the story suggest about the possibilities of forgiveness and healing with people we've written off or given up on, including ourselves?

- What can we take away from Zacchaeus's example of following his heart and responding to God's presence?

- For Jesus to go to Zacchaeus's house meant crossing a strict religious barrier. What boundaries of religion, culture, and ethics might we be asked to cross in order to pursue faith?

- What are some of the economic implications of the story?

- What would it mean to you if Jesus said, "I must come to your house today?"

THE STORY BEHIND THE STORY

Tax collectors, especially chief tax collectors, during Jesus' time were seen as traitors by the Jewish community. They were complicit with the Roman Empire, often paying annual tariffs to Rome in advance and then charging people extra in order to make a profit over and above what they would need to make a normal living. They would sometimes even murder and burn villages in order to intimidate farmers and merchants into paying their taxes. According to both religious ritual and social codes, just by having a tax collector enter one's home put one at risk of not being right with God or one's own social class.

There are some interesting details to this story, beginning with the note about Zacchaeus's stature and that he was running and climbing trees. This, along with the assumption that as a wealthy man he would have been well dressed, conspires to make quite a comical picture. Another detail, that the tree he climbed was a sycamore tree, would have prompted the story's first hearers to recognize a nuance. Sycamores produced figs that were less desirable than other figs and therefore were only eaten by the poor. So here we have a wealthy tax collector getting sticky from the figs of the poor.

In spite of the scene Zacchaeus creates, Jesus is the real focus of the story. He comes up to the tree, calls Zacchaeus by name, and tells him to come down immediately. Jesus says he must stay at Zacchaeus's house. There are no social niceties exchanged. The story shifts from comedy to drama. Suddenly the tone is imperative. This is about a life change and transformation.

The crowd doesn't think it's funny either. Why would Jesus be spending time with someone who is ruining their community?

Furthermore, according to an understanding about religious purity during his time, Jesus could not eat with a tax collector and then worship God in the temple.

In the same chapter of Luke, Jesus enters Jerusalem, where he will die. The urgency in this story is part of the drive towards Jerusalem. In the midst of this urgency, the question of righteousness comes up. A few stories earlier in the gospel Jesus tells of a tax collector and a religious person (Pharisee) praying in the temple. The tax collector is beating his breast in shame, asking for mercy, while the religious person is giving thanks that he's not like the tax collector. Jesus says, "The one who exalts himself will be humbled and the one who humbles himself will be exalted" (18:14). The ones who think themselves righteous are out of the loop, while those who are seen as outside the circle are brought into the center.

Without demanding anything other than hospitality from Zacchaeus, Jesus elicits a remarkable response from the man. Zacchaeus announces that he will give half of his possessions to the poor and pay back four times over anyone he has defrauded. He matches both the standard set by John the Baptist in giving to the poor (whoever has two coats must share with anyone who has none [Luke 3:11]) and the most stringent law of restitution. According to Leviticus 6:5, "You shall repay the principal amount and shall add one-fifth to it. You shall pay it to its owner when you realize your guilt."

The gospel writer shows the power of Jesus' embrace of Zacchaeus's dignity simply as a human being, opening him to change, and bringing justice to his relationships. We discover from the story that the Holy One shows up with urgency and "must stay at our house." God chooses to stand under our tree and to call us by name, seeing in our hearts the desire to be accepted and transformed.

PUSH OUT

Consider the following push outs as ways to further explore the transforming power of God's acceptance.

- Make a list of things for which you want to be forgiven. Include in the list the action steps that would display moving toward freedom and release. Choose one and spend time in reflection, prayer, and discussion with trusted ones on how to move to a different place.

- Create a mask out of cardboard, foil, feathers, yarn, sequins, leaves, construction paper, recycled plastic items, and other things to show components of your true identity trying to get out. Explore in your mask-making what specific parts of your life, personality, or past you seek to have transformed by God's presence.

- The Christian idea of stewardship is about giving of one's resources as a way to express how we "prize" God's goodness. It is an act of joy, just as Zacchaeus responded with joy in giving away his possessions. In praise for what God is doing in your life, carefully consider what percentage of your income you want to give in the next months or year to healing and compassionate work in your local community and the global community. What percentage of your time and energy will you intentionally set aside as a vessel for God's mercy?

- Give some thought to how we in North America actually benefit from the oppression of others. For example, we may buy cheap clothing made by children in sweatshops. We may use cheap gas made possible by the loss of land by poor farmers and indigenous people in other countries. We may have cheap food due to farm subsidies in our countries that make it impossible for others around the world to compete. Engage in conversation with others about what a commitment to economic justice might mean in this context. What can you and others do to work for justice? The Web site for Global Exchange <www.globalexchange.org> is a good resource to help with these discussions and action plans.

- Learn more about hate groups that may be present in your community and efforts to address them. The Anti-Defamation League at <www.adl.org> and the Hate-Crime Network at <www.hate-crime.website-works.com> are two resources toward these efforts.

GROUP IDEAS

[Focus: To receive affirmation of our true character, opening us to the transforming possibilities of God's presence and forgiveness.

LIFE'S A PUSH

- Consider having a collection of masks laid out for participants to try on and play with. If you are in a space that allows, try playing a game of hide-and-seek. Begin by talking a bit about what it's like to hide. What makes it fun? What makes it serious? What are the ways we hide from others or ourselves? What kind of identities do we create to protect ourselves or avoid things?

- Have someone read aloud "Surprising Wisdom" and "The Cantor and the Klansman" and engage the questions provided at the end of "Life's a Push" on page 93.

- Invite participants to share with a partner a personal experience that these stories may have brought to mind.

- Offer the prayer provided on page 93 or a prayer of your own.

THE STORY

- Read the story on page 94 aloud two or three times, pausing in between each reading for a time of silence. Invite several participants to read.

- Choose a method of experiencing the story from the suggestions on page 23. This is a great story to role-play or illustrate because of the interesting characters and details.

YOU PUSH THE STORY

- Discuss possible story pushes using some of the suggestions on page 94 to get things started. List additional pushes on newsprint.

- Have copies of "The Story Behind the Story" on pages 95–96 and invite participants to take a moment to read it. Then discuss the story pushes on page 94.

- Have Bibles available for this section and look at the story's context in Luke, especially chapters 18 and 19. What themes emerge? What insights into the story of Zacchaeus come from the other stories around it?

THE STORY PUSHES YOU

- Have the group list ways the story on page 94 challenges, heals, or gives new perspective. As a guide, refer to the list of questions provided on page 95.

- Give a time of silence for some of these ideas to sink in. Invite participants to journal about one or two of the pushes on page 95 that really speak to their lives.

PUSH OUT

■ Select and complete one or more Push Out experiences from pages 96–97.

■ Offer the prayer below or one of your own in closing.

> **PRAYER**
>
> May we have confidence, O God, that you will continue to come to us in our strength and our vulnerability, our curiosity, and our hiding, seeking us always and everywhere in your mercy. May we find ways to respond in joy and with abundant giving of all that we are and have. Amen.

---

1. Kathryn Watterson, "The Cantor and the Klansman," *Chicken Soup for the Jewish Soul* (Deerfield, Fla.: Health Communications, 2001), 7–13. Used by permission.

9. [ALONE WITH GOD

And he said to them, "I am deeply grieved, even to death; remain here and keep awake."

Mark 14:34

Are there times when everyone seems to abandon you—even God? Here is a glimpse into the humanity of Jesus during a time of betrayal and desertion.

LIFE'S A PUSH

I was faced with having to attend a home-going service for the niece of a dear friend of mine. The loss was sudden, devastating, and disturbing. The girl's best friend had stabbed her over a dispute about some clothes. Neighbors who witnessed the murder left the girl to die on the city street. What a horrible, extreme case of betrayal and abandonment.

Perhaps at one time or another you've felt abandoned by friends or family, people you thought would be there for you. Maybe you've experienced betrayal by a friend in whom you had confided your most intimate thoughts and secrets. Maybe you have been through what the mystics call "the dark night of the soul," when even God seems to have left you alone.

Read here the ancient words of the psalmist in Psalm 22. You may recognize the first verse as the one that Matthew and Mark record Jesus saying from the cross.

> ¹My God, My God, why have you
>   forsaken me?
> Why are you so far from
>   helping me,
>   from the words
>   of my groaning?
> ²O my God, I cry by day, but you
>   do not answer;
>   and by night, but find no rest.

- When have you experienced feelings of abandonment or betrayal? Have they included feeling abandoned by God?
- What does it mean to you that Jesus cried out to God this way from the cross?

ABSENT GOD?

There are times when, whatever I try to do about it and however much I try to resist, whether by trying to lay it down or trying to live with it creatively, the only reality seems to be darkness, emptiness, depression, panic. These times are hard. There is nothing romantic about sleepless nights and colorless days. And God is, or seems to be, absent. As I struggle with this I find that what I most long to do is to shake my fist and shout, "Why me? Why should life be so unfair?"[1]

- Draw or paint a picture, work with clay, or write a poem expressing your own experience with "sleepless nights and colorless days." If you find yourself describing a point of light or a word of hope, what is its source for you?
- Who or what helps you get through these times?

PRAYER

Gracious God, give us patience and courage to move through times of despair, abandonment, and betrayal. Be our breath, our strength, our hope. Make your presence known to us, even in times of feeling your absence. Amen.

THE STORY

Read the story from Mark's Gospel. What new insights, new challenges, or new comforts come to you as you read? What do you learn about Jesus through this story? about the disciples? about God? Consider highlighting the words and phrases that describe the emotions of Jesus or choose a way to experience the story from the suggestions on page 23.

[32]They went to a place called Gethsemane; and he said to his disciples, "Sit here while I pray.
[33]He took with him Peter and James and John, and began to be distressed and agitated. [34]And he said to them, "I am deeply grieved, even unto death; remain here, and keep awake. [35]And going a little farther, he threw himself on the ground and prayed that, if it were possible, the

hour might pass from him. [36]He said, "Abba, Father, for you all things are possible; remove this cup from me; yet, not what I want, but what you want." [37]He came and found them sleeping; and he said to Peter, "Simon, are you asleep? Could you not keep awake one hour? [38]Keep awake and pray that you may not come into the time of trial; the spirit indeed is willing, but the flesh is weak."

[39]And again he went away and prayed, saying the same words. [40]And once more he came and found them sleeping, for their eyes were very heavy; and they did not know what to say to him.

[41]He came a third time and said to them, "Are you still sleeping and taking your rest? Enough! The hour has come; the Son of Man is betrayed into the hands of sinners. [42] Get up, let us be going. See, my betrayer is at hand."

[43]Immediately, while he was still speaking, Judas, one of the twelve, arrived; and with him there was a crown with swords and clubs, from the chief priest, the scribes and the elders. [44]Now the betrayer had given them a sign, saying, "The one I will kiss is the man; arrest him and lead him away under guard." [45]So when he came, he went up to him at once, and said, "Rabbi!" and kissed him. [46]Then they laid hands on him and arrested him. [47]But one of those who stood near drew his sword and struck the slave of the high priest, cutting off his ear. [48]Then Jesus said to them, "Have you come out with swords and clubs to arrest me as though I were a bandit? [49]Day after day I was teaching, and you did not arrest me. But let the scriptures be fulfilled." [50]All of them deserted him and fled.

YOU PUSH THE STORY

How does this story push you? What feelings does it evoke? What do you want to say to the various characters? to God? Bring your questions to the story and work with the following suggestions.

PUSH POSSIBILITIES FOR MARK 14:32–50

- What might Peter, James, and John have been thinking as Jesus took them aside with him to pray? Why were they so sleepy? What did Jesus want or need from them? Why these three?

- What was happening with the other disciples when Jesus took the three off to pray? What might they have been thinking and feeling? Excluded? Relieved? Jealous?

- What do you make of Jesus' prayer? Do you think he believes God wants him to die? Do you believe God wanted him to die?

- In this Gospel, God speaks at Jesus' baptism ("You are my Son, the Beloved; with you I am well pleased" [Mark 1:11]) and at the transfiguration ("This is my Son, the Beloved; listen to him!" [Mark 9:7]). Why is God silent here?

- Jesus says that the scriptures are fulfilled at his arrest. What scriptures?

- Why does everyone abandon Jesus?

- The Garden of Gethsemane, which means the "oil press," was east of Jerusalem near the Mount of Olives. This was the place where olives were crushed and ground. What is the symbolic significance of the setting for this story?

THE STORY PUSHES YOU

Jesus expresses some very real human emotions in this story. Are there any that surprise you? How does the story challenge or support your understanding of Jesus' humanity? Let the story push you about what you believe about Jesus and about the role of friends and God in your own experiences of difficult and lonely struggles.

PUSH POSSIBILITIES FOR MARK 14:32–50

- Does this story make Jesus easier or harder to relate to? Why?

- What would you have done if you had been Peter, James, or John? Judas? One of the other disciples? What would you have prayed if you were Jesus?

- Notice the way Jesus addresses God as, "Abba, Father." How do you address God in times of need? What is your experience of God in difficult times?

- Were you ever called on to be there for a friend through something difficult? Would you change anything about what you did for them?

THE STORY BEHIND THE STORY

The Garden of Gethsemane was an olive grove outside of the wall of Jerusalem on the way to the Mount of Olives. It was on the Mount of Olives that Jesus predicted terrible events awaiting all who follow him (Mark 13:3–13) and even the loss of his disciples (Mark 14:27). Jesus, sensing that the events leading to the fulfillment of those predictions, as well as to his own death, are about to unfold, goes to a quiet place to pray. Only three times in Mark's Gospel is Jesus portrayed as praying. Once near the beginning of his ministry (1:35), once in the middle

(6:46), and now here toward the end. Jesus takes with him the three disciples who are the "inner circle" in Mark's Gospel (5:37; 9:2). Jesus tells them to keep watch, reiterating a theme of his ministry (8:15; 13:5; 13:34–37). But as readers of this Gospel know, the disciples have a reputation for promising faith and fidelity with seemingly little understanding of the real costs (10:35–39).

In the garden, Jesus leaves even the inner circle of his disciples, staggering under the enormous weight of what he must now bear alone. Clearly in verses 34 and 35 Jesus is in deep emotional distress. The hour that he pleads with God about, which he spoke of in 13:32, has now come. And the cup, representative of the suffering he now knows he will have to endure, is the cup he spoke of in 10:38–39.

Following the third time Jesus wakes his disciples, later to be echoed in Peter's three-fold denial of Jesus in 14:66–72, the long-awaited clash between Jesus and the temple authorities comes. Like many totalitarian regimes, the authorities come heavily armed and under the cover of night, even though Jesus has no weapons or guards and is not in hiding. Jesus makes no particular references when he says that his arrest is a fulfillment of scripture. Some scholars suggest a reference is being made to Isaiah 53:12: "Therefore I will allot him a portion with the great, and he shall divide the spoil with the strong; because he poured out himself to death and was numbered with the transgressors; yet he bore the sin of many, and made intercession for the transgressors." (The Gospel of Matthew is slightly more specific, naming the "scriptures of the prophets" [Matthew 26:55] but still not making this direct link.)

All through Mark's Gospel Jesus identifies himself as "Son of Man." This might be better translated as "the human one." The author of Mark takes pains to make sure readers understand that Jesus is a human being. Nowhere is the humanity of Jesus more evident than in this scene so marked by vulnerability and fear.

PUSH OUT

This is an important story in that it chronicles events leading up to the death and resurrection of Jesus, the heart of the Christian tradition. But this is also an amazing story for the way it brings us right up close to the very humanity of Jesus. To know that Jesus experienced the grip of despair, feelings of abandonment, and the sting of betrayal is to not feel so entirely alone with our own similar experiences. There are times when we just have to reach out for help. Here are some suggestions for getting through the "dark night of the soul" and for helping others do the same:

- Many local communities have grief-support services and bereavement organizations. You might speak to a pastor for recommendations about these or for pastoral counseling referrals.

- For information on depression and other mental health issues, go to <www.nmha.org>.

- Keep a prayer journal. As this will be a completely private resource, express your concerns and feelings to God as honestly as possible. Let it be a raw account of your struggles, doubts, hopes, and celebrations. Instead of writing some of the entries, draw or paint them.

- Read all of Psalm 22. From where and to where does the psalm travel? Where are you on the journey? What gives you hope?

- What might it mean for you to join with others to keep vigil for human rights? The following Web sites provide information about opportunities to get involved in important ministries of solidarity and keeping watch:

  - Human Rights Watch <www.hrw.org>: An advocacy group that also offers updated human rights news.

  - Amnesty International <www.amnesty.org>: Local projects, events, and publications, as well as international updates on human rights and organizations' activities.

  - Keston Institute <www.keston.org/persecutionframe.htm>: Monitors freedom of religion and offers contact information for correspondence with officials, as well as lists of prisoners of conscience affiliated with many faiths in many countries.

- The following books may be helpful to you or others in dealing with grief and loss. This selection covers a broad range of theological and ideological viewpoints—find those that are most comfortable for you. Ask your pastor or a counselor for other suggestions: *When Bad Things Happen to Good People* (New York: Schocken, 1989) by Harold S. Kushner, *A Grief Observed* (San Francisco: HarperSanFrancisco, 2001) by C. S. Lewis, and *Out of the Ashes: A Handbook for Starting Over* (New York: Paulist Press, 1997) by Patrick J. McDonald and Claudette M. McDonald.

GROUP IDEAS   [Focus: To journey with Jesus
                         through struggle and
                         abandonment.

Life's a Push

- Create a comforting environment for this session. Soft lighting, pillows on the floor, quiet, meditative music playing. Bring or ask others to bring art supplies (paints, markers, paper, clay, etc.).

- Read this section and discuss the questions provided on page 101.

- Engage in the suggested art activity.

The Story

- Read Mark 14:32–50. Ask group members to write about what they think Jesus was thinking and feeling.

- Choose a way to experience the story from pages 17–23.

You Push the Story

- Discuss the push possibilities on pages 102–103.

The Story Pushes You

- Choose one or more of the push possibilities on page 103 to discuss as a group.

- Invite the group to illustrate the ways they address God in prayer in difficult times, using the art supplies.

Push Out

- Go over the push out suggestions with the group. What recommendations can group members share with each other for support services in your area?

- Visit one of the human rights Web sites. Plan a way to become involved in the work of the organization as a group.

- Close with Psalm 121 using "God" or "the Lord," as you choose, or a prayer of your own.

PRAYER

¹I lift up my eyes to the hills—
    from whence does my help come?
²My help comes from God [or The Lord],
    who made heaven and earth.

³God will not let your foot be moved;
    the one who keeps you will not slumber;
⁴the one who keeps Israel
    will neither slumber nor sleep.

God [or The Lord] is your keeper;
    God [or The Lord] is your shade
    on your right hand.
⁶The sun shall not smite you by day,
    nor the moon by night.
God [or The Lord] will keep you from all evil,
    and will keep your life.
⁸God [or The Lord] will keep
    your going out and your coming in
    from this time forth and forevermore.²

1. Esther de Waal, *Living with Contradiction: Reflections on the Rule of St. Benedict* (San Francisco: Harper San Francisco, 1989), 118.

2. *An Inclusive Language Lectionary: Readings for Year B, rev. ed.* (Atlanta, Ga.: John Knox Press; New York: The Pilgrim Press; Philadelphia: The Westminister Press, 1987), 192.

10. [IT'S NOT OVER 'TIL IT'S OVER

"Don't be alarmed," he said. "You are looking for Jesus the Nazarene, who was crucified. He has been raised. He is not here. See the place where they laid him. But go, tell his disciples and Peter, 'He is going ahead of you into Galilee. There you will see him, just as he told you.'"

Mark 16.1–8

When Jesus went ahead of the disciples into Galilee, he invited them into a story that has not yet ended. What does it mean for us as twenty-first-century disciples to be invited into this "never-ending" story of following Jesus?

 LIFE'S A PUSH

THIS IS THE END

The end. The End. THE END. It seems so simple, short, and sweet. But think of all the ways "the end" is anything but simple. How many times have you been annoyed by someone who is telling a riveting story or great joke only to pause and say, "Oh, man, I can't remember how it ends." Or who among us has not run screaming from the room, with hands over our ears, saying, "Don't tell me how it ends. I haven't seen it yet!" Or maybe you are the opposite. When no one is looking, you sneak a glance at the last page of the book, unable to wait to know who did what to whom, how, and why.

Endings. Every speech-giver and performer knows the beginning can be shaky, the middle so-so, but if the ending is great, that's what they'll remember. And how many times do you hear, "I think it should have ended differently"? You never hear much said about things starting differently.

Everyone knows it's not where you start, it's where you finish. And no one will argue with Olympian John Stephen Akhwari of Tanzania, the last-place finisher in the marathon at Mexico City's 1968 Olympic Games, when he said, "My country did not send me to Mexico City to start the race. They sent me here to finish."

There is something compelling about finishing what we start. But in God's work in the world, we may not be called to be finishers. Are we open to the possibility that we might be starting in the middle of something bigger than ourselves, something that has been going on for a few millennia and may go on for more? Can we be as excited about following as we are about finishing?

- What is your favorite ending to a story or movie? Why?

- Recall a time when it was oh-so-difficult for you to start something, but then you were oh-so-excited about the way it ended.

- Describe a time when you were so into something you were involved in that you didn't want it to end.

When was the last time you said, "It's not over yet"? What did you mean by that? Did you wish it were over, or were you glad it wasn't?

I WILL FOLLOW

How does this song by Kelly S. Moor resonate with your sense of call to follow Jesus? If you ranked how fitting the song is to describe your faith journey, what number would you give it? A "1" because it doesn't fit at all or a "5" because it fits you "to a T"? somewhere in between? What would you like to ask or say to Jesus about what it means to follow him?

> Sometimes I don't know You.
> Sometimes I don't recognize Your face.
> Sometimes rough clouds appear,
> and I cannot walk in faith.
> But you are the One
> I hear calling in my dreams:
> "Come and Follow."
> Will You lead me?
> I want to believe!
> So take my hand.
> Walk here by my side.
> Sometimes I'm afraid,
> but I will follow where you lead.
> Through all my days and nights,
> from darkness into light.
> I will follow where you lead.

Life is full of journeys.
Sometimes I feel lost and out of place.
Sometimes no path is clear,
And I have to walk by faith.
But you are the One I hear calling in my heart:
"Come and Follow." Will you lead me?
I want to believe!
So take my hand.[1]

PRAYER

Eternal God, we ask for your guidance as we move through the middle, as we seek to be faithful in the midst of everyday life. It helps to know you've been here before us and are with us still, all along the way. Help us not to try to get ahead of you. Amen.

Though this is the ending of the Gospel of Mark, for the disciples faced with the empty tomb, it is the beginning of a new way of following Jesus.

THE STORY

Read together with the group the story from Mark 16.1–8 or select a method of sharing from "Bible Experience ideas" on page 23.

[1]When the Sabbath was over, Mary Magdalene, Mary the mother of James, and Salome bought spices so that they might go to anoint Jesus' body. [2]Very early on the first day of the week, just after sunrise, they were on their way to the tomb [3]and they asked each other, "Who will roll the stone away from the entrance of the tomb?"

[4]But when they looked up, they saw that the stone, which was very large, had been rolled away. [5]As they entered the tomb, they saw a young man dressed in a white robe sitting on the right side, and they were alarmed.

[6]"Don't be alarmed," he said. "You are looking for Jesus the Nazarene, who was crucified. He has risen. He is not here. See the place where they laid him. [7]But go, tell his disciples and Peter, 'He is going ahead of you into Galilee. There you will see him, just as he told you.'"

[8]Trembling and bewildered, the women went out and fled from the tomb. They said nothing to anyone, because they were afraid.

YOU PUSH THE STORY

For generations those who have studied Mark's Gospel have had questions about the abrupt way it seems to end. The women, surprised by finding a stranger in the tomb rather than the body of Jesus, must have been filled with questions. The gospel writer says that they were amazed and afraid. The disciples who heard the women's report no doubt had their questions, too. Push the story by adding your own questions to the ones below.

PUSH POSSIBILITIES FOR MARK 16:1–8

- Many Bible translations include two alternative endings to this gospel. Would you have ended the gospel with 16:8? Do you think it's abrupt? What purpose do you think the gospel writer had in mind for ending it this way?

- Who was the young man in the white robe? A figment of the women's imagination? A messenger from God? Someone who wandered into the tomb for a good night's sleep? Does it make a difference who he is?

- Why were the women bringing spices to put on the body when Jesus told them he would rise after three days? What might they have been thinking and feeling after all that had just happened?

- Why are the women afraid at the tomb?

- According to this original ending, the women don't tell their story. How do we know it today?

- What is significant about the stone having been rolled away?

- Why do you think the women are given a message for Peter and the disciples rather than the message being given to the men directly?

- Does this passage feel to you like an "end" to the story of the life of Jesus? Why or why not?

THE STORY PUSHES YOU

The message the young man had for the disciples is an intriguing one: Jesus was going ahead of them into Galilee. It nudges us to consider the implications of Christ preceding us into the places we are going and calling us to follow. This can be both a comforting and discomforting idea. Christ may be asking us to go some places we hadn't considered before, to do the work of God's realm, bringing peace and justice to the oppressed and giving of ourselves in ways we didn't believe possible.

- What does the idea that Christ precedes you into any situation mean to you?

- What things that you know about the teachings and actions of Jesus might give you an idea of places you may be asked to go or things you may be asked to do?

- Can you identify with the way the women just run away and say nothing to anyone?

THE STORY BEHIND THE STORY

It is generally accepted that Mark's is the first of the four Gospels to have been written. While the date is not certain, it was probably completed before the fall of Jerusalem in 70 CE. Most likely the author collected stories from the oral traditions about Jesus and from several collections of sayings that were already in existence. Just who was the author is still an open question: the name "Mark" was common, and there is no certain evidence in the gospel or in other texts that would identify the author specifically.

Mark's Gospel is the only Gospel to actually call itself a gospel (1:1). The original nuance of the word "gospel" is more "glad tidings" or "joyous cry" than simply the "good news" we know today. A quick shout is the effect of Mark's style: short, vivid, and intense. As this is the earliest gospel, the audience is so close in time to the events that are recounted that Mark does not need to explain all the details of customs and traditions. For example, he can say that the women were taking spices to anoint Jesus' body, and people would understand that. He could raise the issue of the stone, knowing that his readers would have understood that the stone could be rolled back and forth, as these tombs were reused many times. He quickly dismisses the possibility that the body had been removed by having the young man proclaim what has happened.

There is some debate among scholars about the ending of this Gospel. You'll notice in some versions of the Bible, such as the New Revised Standard Version, there are two additional sentences added on to verse 8 called the shorter ending of Mark. Also, verses 9–20 of chapter 16 are labeled, "The Longer Ending of Mark." Most scholars argue that the Gospel ends with the first section of verse 8. The purpose of Mark's Gospel was to encourage the church to step into the story and begin to complete the work that Jesus and the disciples had begun. Ending with Jesus going on ahead invites disciples to follow. As Lamar Williamson Jr. has written, "Mark's ending is no end; only the reader can bring closure."[2] This is true for the original readers, for us, and for all future readers.

Why Galilee? Why does the Gospel end with Jesus going ahead of the disciples to Galilee? Galilee was where Jesus began his ministry. The disciples are called back to the beginning. They will now proclaim the good news of God's realm just as Jesus had. They will be the presence of Christ in the world.

PUSH OUT

A small group of disciples and followers of Jesus have grown into a global church whose impact on the world has been great if not always positive. Those of us who follow Christ now have opportunity to live new chapters into the unfinished story of Mark 16. Consider some of the following ideas for discovering ways you can continue the story.

- Women were the first to be sent to tell others the good news of Jesus' resurrection and to give them Jesus' instructions. Yet there are those who would deny women that opportunity today. How active is your faith community in encouraging all people to respond to the call to follow Jesus in all ways, whether as professional clergy or in other vocations? Interview some women clergy in your area to find out what kind of obstacles they have faced in their professional journeys and how they discerned and followed their calling.

- "Finish" the Gospel of Mark by writing several verses that narrate what you think happened with the women and the disciples.

- Imagine the history of God's work on earth as a sweep of color and lines. Draw and color what you imagine, and place yourself into that history. List some words that describe how you imagine your tasks in God's work. Add words that describe how you feel to be a part of God's story in the world.

- Identify talents, abilities, and interests you have that God might use in advancing the work of God's realm. Discuss with a friend, church leader, or someone you respect who is doing work you'd like to do how you might get involved in something that applies your gifts to God's purposes.

**GROUP IDEAS**   [Focus: To discover how we participate in the "rest of the story" of following Jesus.

LIFE'S A PUSH

■ Ask the group to suggest changes to well-known endings, like *Gone with the Wind, Romeo and Juliet, Cruel Intentions,* the lives of Kurt Cobain or James Dean, or other contemporary examples.

■ Discuss together the questions found on page 109.

■ Ask a volunteer to read the lyrics to the song "I Will Follow" or sing it if you know it.

■ Pray together the prayer on page 110 or one of your own.

THE STORY

■ Read aloud the story from Mark 16:1–8 or select as a group one of the "Bible Experiences for Young Adults" suggestions on page 23.

YOU PUSH THE STORY

■ Ask a member of the group to review the resurrection stories of the four Gospels and to make a chart showing the similarities and differences in the accounts or make copies of the resurrection passages from a gospel-parallel book and distribute to the group. Discuss the different endings. What impact does each ending have?

■ Allow time for the group members to come up with any of their own pushes and to discuss them along with the push possibilities found on page 111.

THE STORY PUSHES YOU

■ Allow members of the group to review and discuss the push possibilities on page 112 and identify any other ways they are being pushed by this story.

PUSH OUT

■ Be prepared with the resources and materials suggested on page 113. Ask the group which of the ideas they might like to try. Let them come up with their own suggestions. Choose one or two to experience together.

■ As a closing prayer, learn with the group the song "I Will Follow" by Kelly S. Moor on pages 109–110.

1.   Kelly S. Moor, "I Will Follow," *Take a Stand: 23 Songs to Make a Better World* (Carlsbad, Calif.: Better World Artists and Activists Guild and the American Baptist Board of Education and Publication, 1996), 24.
2.   Lamar Williamson Jr,. *Mark*, Interpretation (Atlanta, Ga.: John Knox Press, 1983).

11. [MAY I HAVE YOUR ATTENTION, PLEASE?

Now as he was going along and approaching Damascus, suddenly a light from heaven flashed around him. He fell to the ground and heard a voice saying to him, "Saul, Saul, why do you persecute me?"

Acts 9:1–19a

> How do we determine if happenings in our lives are God's attempts to get our attention? If they are, how do we respond to them?

LIFE'S A PUSH

LIGHTENING BOLT OR WHISPER?

Your mother speaks your *entire* name—first, middle (she promised never to say it in public), and last. The leggy model in the shortest of shorts is poised on the hood of the car whispering, "Going my way?" from the safe distance of the TV screen. The jumbo headline on the cover of a glossy magazine reads: ARE YOU SEXY ENOUGH TO GET HIM? TO KEEP HIM? The giant arrow made of glaring yellow lights at the car lot declares, "We will change your life!" Or how about the ever-popular tabloid headline that reads, UFO CAPTURES HOLLYWOOD!

From giant computer-generated billboards to the symphony of cellular-phone rings, someone is always trying to get our attention. Often people are trying to get us to buy into a new way of thinking or a new mode of doing something, changing our minds as much as making a purchase. It's not unusual for a person or a company to resort to extraordinary measures to get our attention. Whatever it takes, someone out there is willing to do it to make us sit up and take notice.

It's not just about advertising and clever slogans. In the Middle East, a car bomb is detonated in a crowded shopping area. In Eastern Europe, people desperate for medical help watch as a Red Cross ambulance is shelled and their hopes for aid explode in fire and pandemonium. In the United States, the World Trade Center Towers and the Pentagon building are bombed with hijacked passenger planes. If someone wants attention badly enough they will find a way to get it.

When we are babies, we learn to get someone's attention by crying. More often than not, somebody rushes to find out what's the matter. As we grow up we learn that other people have ways of getting *our* attention. When a parent calls us by our full name, they are expecting a different kind of response than when they use our nickname. If one of our boisterous friends seems unusually quiet, she probably wants us to really listen. Or when the quiet one actually raises his voice, we'd better hear what he is saying.

■   What are one or two sure-fire ways that someone can get your attention?

■   Design an advertising hook for your favorite product or an imagined product. Why do you think people would respond to it?

■   Do you believe that God intervenes in our lives to get our attention? If so, how?

PRAYER

Holy God, help us to be attentive to you. We offer you all the ways we have of knowing: all our senses, our intuition, our open minds, and our hearts. Amen.

THE STORY

The Bible tells any number of stories about God's trying to get people's attention. In an act that's surely hard to follow, even with today's sophisticated advertising tricks and wonders, God spoke from a flaming bush to Moses. With Jonah God had to enlist an enormous fish. Once God even resorted to "a bolt out of the blue." Read the Bible story from Acts 9:1–19a or choose a method of engaging the story from the Bible Experience ideas on page 23.

¹Meanwhile Saul, still breathing threats and murder against the disciples of the Lord, went to the high priest ²and asked him for letters to the synagogues at Damascus, so that if he found any who belonged to the Way, men or women, he might bring them bound to Jerusalem. ³Now as he was going along and approaching Damascus, suddenly a light from heaven flashed around him. ⁴He fell to the ground and heard a voice saying to him, "Saul, Saul, why do you persecute me?" ⁵He asked, "Who are you, Lord?" The reply came, "I am Jesus, whom you are persecuting. ⁶But get up and enter the city, and you will be told what you are to do." ⁷The men who were traveling with him stood speechless because they heard the voice but saw no one. ⁸Saul got up from the ground, and

though his eyes were open, he could see nothing; so they led him by the hand and brought him into Damascus. ⁹For three days he was without sight, and neither ate nor drank.

¹⁰Now there was a disciple in Damascus named Ananias. The Lord said to him in a vision, "Ananias." He answered, "Here I am, Lord." ¹¹The Lord said to him, "Get up and go to the street called Straight, and at the house of Judas look for a man of Tarsus named Saul. At this moment he is praying, ¹²and he has seen in a vision a man named Ananias come in and lay his hands on him so he might regain his sight." ¹³But Ananias answered, "Lord, I have heard from many about this man, how much evil he has done to your saints in Jerusalem; ¹⁴and here he has authority from the chief priests to bind all who invoke your name." ¹⁵But the Lord said to him, "Go, for he is an instrument whom I have chosen to bring my name before Gentiles and kings and before the people of Israel; ¹⁶I myself will show him how much he must suffer for the sake of my name."

¹⁷So Ananias went and entered the house. He laid his hands on Saul and said, "Brother Saul, the Lord Jesus, who appeared to you on your way here, has sent me so that you may regain your sight and be filled with the Holy Spirit." ¹⁸And immediately something like scales fell from his eyes, and his sight was restored. Then he got up and was baptized, ¹⁹and after taking some food, he regained his strength.

YOU PUSH THE STORY

Are there things about this story that confuse you? Is there anything in the way God acts in this story that makes you feel reassured? That unsettles you? Push this story with some of these or your own questions.

PUSH POSSIBILITIES FOR ACTS 9:1–19A

- Do you feel that Saul should have been punished for persecuting everyone as he did? Why or why not?

- Why did God choose someone like Saul to be God's messenger, when there must have been other people—like the disciples and other followers—who had better qualifications?

- Why did God get Saul's attention in such a dramatic way?

- What might have been going through Saul's head for those three days?

- Compare God's message to Saul with God's message to Ananias. What is God asking of each of them?

- Ananias was brought to attention by God's instruction to minister to Saul. What kind of changes in attitude did he experience in order to obey God? Do you think there was a lasting transformation?

THE STORY PUSHES YOU

The story pushes us in at least three ways: it raises questions about God's attention-getting role in our lives, it invites us to consider what messages God may be trying to get across to us, and it asks us to consider that we ourselves may actually be the way that God communicates with others.

PUSH POSSIBILITIES FOR ACTS 9:1–19A

- What circumstances bring God to mind for you? Are you more likely to experience God's presence in nature? Through relationships? In your own reflections during times of quiet? In "bolts out of the blue?"

- What keeps you from seeing or hearing what God might be trying to say to you?

- Both Saul and Ananias were asked to give up opinions they held strongly. Has God ever asked the same of you? What were the circumstances?

- Ananias had to be convinced before he went to see a notorious persecutor of believers. Who would you have to be convinced to go to talk to about God?

- Have you ever "shared grace" with someone? How did it happen? What moved you to do that? What are some ways that we can be involved in restoring people in our communities?

THE STORY BEHIND THE STORY

This story is actually one of three accounts of the same incident in the book of Acts. Each one adds detail to the others. We learn, for example, in Acts 22:9 that Paul's companions at the time "saw the light, but they did not understand the voice of the one who was speaking." In this version Ananias has the additional responsibility of telling Saul that he—Saul—has been called by God. Ananias, so afraid of Paul earlier, here tells him rather curtly, "And now what are you waiting for? Get up, be baptized and wash your sins away." The third account in Acts 22:9–18 adds an extended response by God to Paul's question, "Who are you?" Here God tells Saul directly and immediately that he has been chosen to proclaim God's message. Ananias doesn't appear at all. The author of the Gospel of Luke and Acts uses repetition to emphasize key points, and the conversion of Saul is certainly a key point in the development of the church and in the writing of the New Testament.

Born in Tarsus and trained as a Pharisee—a Jewish leader who interpreted and taught the law—Saul verged on the fanatic in his persecution of Christian-Jewish believers before his conversion. He believed sincerely in the Hebrew Scriptures and thought that the Christian movement was dangerous to the Jewish faith. His first appearance in the Bible, Acts 7:58, tells of his complicity in the stoning death of the Christian leader Stephen. Saul's teacher Gamaliel had urged his fellow leaders to allow the sect of Christianity a chance to prove itself within the Jewish community. We read in Acts 5:38–39 his words:

> Therefore, in this present case I advise you: Leave these men alone! Let them go! For if their purpose or activity is of human origin, it will fail. But if it is from God, you will not be able to stop these men; you will only find yourselves fighting against God.

But Saul's zealotry wasn't diminished by this admonition. He was on his way to Damascus with permission from some Jewish religious leaders to capture believers and return them 150 miles to Jerusalem for punishment when God stopped him in his tracks.

Tradition has it that Saul eventually abandoned his name, the name of the first king of Israel, which means "asked" and adopted "Paul," meaning "little one," as a reflection of the humility he felt despite his growing fame and authority within the sect he once persecuted. Scriptures give no account of this tradition, however. Paul spent the rest of his life preaching the gospel of Christ with the same devotion and vehemence he had earlier given its persecution. The thirteen New Testament letters, or epistles, attributed to him lay the foundation for much of Christian theology. And in a reversal of his early unwillingness to accept any new way of thinking in regards to his faith, Paul helped convince the Jewish believers of Christ that Gentiles were acceptable to God and should also be acceptable to them.

Although he played a key role in getting Paul started in ministry and he himself had to have his mind changed by a vision from God, Ananias does not appear in the New Testament other than in the first two accounts of Saul's conversion in Acts. It is not unusual in biblical storytelling that a character crucial to a plotline be introduced for that specific role, only to disappear from the story.

Note the term "the Way," used to describe the early followers of Christ in the book of Acts (it appears six more times). The term less likely comes from Jesus' identification of himself as "the way, the truth, and the life" in John 14:6 than from the believers' own understanding that they were preparing a way for the return of Christ.

PUSH OUT

The story of the Lord's commanding Saul's attention on the way to Damascus— and Ananias's attention in a vision—suggests that God is trying to communicate with us in many and varied ways and that God may be wanting to use us to communicate God's message to other people. God's message is often that we need to reconsider some of our most cherished opinions or change some of our most common behaviors. Ananias was willing to reconsider the fear that made him resist going to restore Saul's sight. He became the messenger of healing to Saul. One can wonder if Saul spent the three days without sight reflecting on his persecution of the people of the Way. He certainly reconsidered his life and became the messenger of God's grace to the entire Mediterranean region. Perhaps some of the following can help you identify God's media and God's messages to you and to those around you.

- Watch the movie *American History X* (New Line Studios; dir. Tony Kaye, 1998). The main character experiences a dramatic change in perspective because of something happening in his life. If you watch the film with others, discuss the nature of his change and what prompts it. Also, how does the character influence others with his change?

- Activists operate in many arenas, hoping that people will take notice and begin to examine the status quo and consider new, different, and perhaps better ways of interacting with people, governments, and nature. Look on some of the following Web sites for perspectives that might differ from your own. If you have the opportunity, discuss some of the issues with other interested persons.

    <www.firstmonday.org/issues/issue4_12/cisler/index.html> the World Trade Organization

    <www.feminist.org/research/report/102_one.html> treatment of women by the Taliban

<http://earthwatch.unep.net/> environmental issue updates

<www.geocities.com/Athens/Delphi/1088/natives/english.htm> the threat to bilingual education in areas where American Indians are schooled

<www.wcl.american.edu/hrbrief/v5i1/html/migrant.html> treatment of migrant workers in the United States

- Passionate people who are converted in dramatic ways often become even more passionate in their new beliefs. Malcolm X once said, "My whole life has been a chronology of changes." Read *The Autobiography of Malcolm X.* A brief recounting of Malcolm's life by Zameer Baber in an article "From Malcolm X to El Hajj El Shabazz," can be found at <www.unix-ag.uni-kl.de/~moritz/malcolm.html/>. Click on "X Quotes."

- Many of the hymns of the church speak of a changed life—sometimes based on a moment of attending to God's message in a startling new way. Look at some of the hymns listed below in a denominational hymnal or look them up online. Have you had the type of turn-around experiences they proclaim? Consider writing a new stanza for any of these songs that tells the story of your own change in attitude, behavior, belief, or perspective.

  "Amazing Grace"

  "Pass It On"

  "Here I Am, Lord"

- Identify someone who was an Ananias to you. Perhaps this person brought you comfort or good news just when you needed it. Maybe they challenged your assumptions, helped you see something in a new way. They might have helped to shape your faith by showing you new ways of thinking. Contact that person and thank them for their actions and caring toward you.

- Saul became a catalyst for the spreading of the Christian faith only after Ananias gave up his fear and reluctance to have anything to do with him. Is there an individual from whom you have kept your distance for some reason or another? Try to determine your reason for doing so. Then offer that reason to God in prayer and ask for a change of heart. Believing that God is faithful to answer your prayer, consider ways you could connect or reconnect with that person.

GROUP IDEAS

[Focus: To reflect on ways God may be trying to get our attention.

LIFE'S A PUSH

- Gather a selection of bizarre headlines, advertisements, or campaign slogans that really try hard to capture people's attention. Post them around the gathering space.

- Read together "Lightening Bolt or Whisper" on pages 115–116 and invite participants to discuss the questions.

- Distribute paper and colored pencils or markers with which to design advertising hooks. Allow time for each participant to create and share his or her design.

- Pray the prayer provided on page 116 or one of your own.

THE STORY

- Read Acts 9:1–19a or select for your group another way to experience the story from page 23.

- Ask several people to read God's lines from the story on pages 116–117. Discuss how to portray God. Angry? Hurt? Frustrated? Out of patience?

- Bring to the group copies of some of the famous paintings of the conversion of Paul. Better-known works available from the Internet include those by Caravaggio (1600), Bruegel (mid 1550s), and the striking 1991 piece by Francis Hoyland. What do group members think each artist is trying to convey?

YOU PUSH THE STORY

- Encourage the group to share any questions or confusions that arise from the story.

- Invite the group to review the push possibilities on pages 117–118 and to discuss them.

THE STORY PUSHES YOU

- Discuss the push possibilities on page 118. What other ways are people in the group being pushed by the story?

PUSH OUT

- Choose one or more of the push possibilities on pages 120–121 to do together as a group. Also encourage members to complete the individual activities on their own.

- Ask members of the group to offer the names of persons who were Ananiases to them. When everyone has had an opportunity, ask someone to lead in a prayer of thanksgiving for those people.

- Choose a hymn such as those listed previously or "Change My Heart, O God," from *New Song: Musical Expressions, 1st ed.* (Louisville, Ky.: Presbyterian Church (U.S.A.), 1998), 30; or "Won't You Let Me Be Your Servant" from *The Chalice Hymnal* (St. Louis, Mo.: Chalice Press, 1995), 539, to close the session.

12. [LIVING FAITH OUT LOUD

At the same hour of the night he took them and washed
their wounds; then he and his entire family were baptized
without delay.

Acts 16:33

> Acting out faith publicly can bring rejection and
> hardship as well as new opportunities to discover
> God's transforming power. Several early church
> leaders encounter both rejection and hospitality
> in following God's Spirit.

LIFE'S A PUSH

Wearing a cross can be fashionable. But actually professing a faith can get some
negative reactions. A young woman was accepted to three medical schools and was
trying to decide which one to go to. After a trip to Honduras with her church, she
decided that she was being led to study theology and maybe become a church professional. When she announced her decision to her friends, some of them asked,
"Are you sure you want to do that? What about medical school?"

Often religious people are portrayed as nice, private folks, good citizens who
don't rock the boat. Maintaining that image becomes a little more difficult when
you discover that what you believe requires you to challenge some things that are
going on in the world. Sometimes simply living compassionate, open lives can
bring us into conflict with a majority opinion, with our own government, or with
something we have previously accepted without question. One trip with a friend
to criminal court, one encounter with someone who cannot find adequate day care
for his or her children, one family member who experiences neglect or ill treatment from a mental health care system, or one friend who is treated unjustly by
civil authorities can lead us on a surprising journey of witnessing to the truth in
bold and public ways.

- What decisions have you made based on your faith that were called into question by others around you? How did you respond?

- Have there been times when your understanding of where God is leading you
  has caused you to come into conflict with an accepted way of doing things,
  "the system," a law, or what your family has always believed?

124

GOD'S PEACE IN A TORTURE CHAMBER

A religious activist for human rights in Colombia makes frequent trips to North America to tell his story. The first time he made the trip in 1977 he was detained by authorities. The activist, who must remain anonymous for security reasons, spoke of that experience to a community organization in Syracuse, New York, recently:

> I was shoved to the floor, the only thing I could think of was committing suicide to escape more hangings and blows. The radio station blurted out the Bible story of Daniel in the pit with the lions. (Detained soldiers in the next cell turned the radio to an evangelical station to avoid being caught smoking drugs.) Hearing this passage from Daniel, I was filled with a sense of security and tranquility. When I woke up, my cousin arrived and asked to see me. The soldiers bathed me and gave me stale bread; the torture ended and they took me before a military judge who sent me to jail from the torture center. That Easter Day I celebrated by naming my first child Daniel. And every time people lift their voices and take to the streets to fight for drinking water, for control over oil production, for a little control in their lives, I live Easter. When the people rise together it is like the light of lightning in the night.

- Like this activist many people experience the presence of God in the midst of their struggles in the political realm. What is your experience with this way of living the faith? What are your impressions of it?

- When have you sensed God's empowering presence in the midst of hardship?

PRAYER

O Holy One, may we perceive your guiding presence in the very midst of our decisions and struggles, in the people we meet, the situations we encounter, the causes we champion. Give us the courage to follow where you lead. Amen.

Early church leaders lived their faith in the public arena, incurring the wrath of some and winning the hearts of others. The story for today resounds with their boldness. They followed courageously where they believed God was leading them.

THE STORY

Read the Bible story from the Acts of the Apostles. Then choose a method of experiencing the story from those listed on page 23. One suggestion is to read the passage and mark with a highlighter or underline where the power shifts from one group or person to others. This is also a wonderful story to act out or pantomime.

¹³On the sabbath day we went outside the gate by the river, where we supposed there was a place of prayer; and we sat down and spoke to the women who had gathered there. ¹⁴A certain woman named Lydia, a worshiper of God, was listening to us; she was from the city of Thyatira and a dealer in purple cloth. The Lord opened her heart to listen eagerly to what was said by Paul. ¹⁵When she and her household were baptized, she urged us, saying, "If you have judged me to be faithful to the Lord, come and stay at my home." And she prevailed upon us.

¹⁶One day, as we were going to the place of prayer, we met a slave-girl who had a spirit of divination and brought her owners a great deal of money by fortune-telling. ¹⁷While she followed Paul and us, she would cry out, "These men are slaves of the Most High God, who proclaim to you a way of salvation." ¹⁸She kept doing this for many days. But Paul, very much annoyed, turned and said to the spirit, "I order you in the name of Jesus Christ to come out of her." And it came out that very hour.

¹⁹But when her owners saw that their hope of making money was gone, they seized Paul and Silas and dragged them into the marketplace before the authorities. ²⁰When they had brought them before the magistrates, they said, "These men are disturbing our city; they are Jews ²¹and are advocating customs that are not lawful for us as Romans to adopt or observe." ²²The crowd joined in attacking them, and the magistrates had them stripped of their clothing and ordered them to be beaten with rods. ²³After they had given them a severe flogging, they threw them into prison and ordered the jailer to keep them securely. ²⁴Following these instructions, he put them in the innermost cell and fastened their feet in the stocks.

²⁵About midnight Paul and Silas were praying and singing hymns to God, and the prisoners were listening to them. ²⁶Suddenly there was an earthquake, so violent that the foundations of the prison were shaken; and immediately all the doors were opened and everyone's chains were unfastened. ²⁷When the jailer woke up and saw the prison doors wide

open, he drew his sword and was about to kill himself, since he supposed that the prisoners had escaped. [28]But Paul shouted in a loud voice, "Do not harm yourself, for we are all here." [29]The jailer called for lights, and rushing in, he fell down trembling before Paul and Silas. [30]Then he brought them outside and said, "Sirs, what must I do to be saved?" [31]They answered, "Believe on the Lord Jesus, and you will be saved, you and your household." [32]They spoke the word of the Lord to him and to all who were in his house. [33]At the same hour of the night he took them and washed their wounds; then he and his entire family were baptized without delay. [34]He brought them up into the house and set food before them; and he and his entire household rejoiced that he had become a believer in God.

[35]When morning came, the magistrates sent the police, saying, "Let those men go." [36]And the jailer reported the message to Paul, saying, "The magistrates sent word to let you go; therefore come out now and go in peace." [37]But Paul replied, "They have beaten us in public, uncondemned, men who are Roman citizens, and have thrown us into prison; and now are they going to discharge us in secret? Certainly not! Let them come and take us out themselves." [38]The police reported these words to the magistrates, and they were afraid when they heard that they were Roman citizens; [39]so they came and apologized to them. And they took them out and asked them to leave the city. [40]After leaving the prison they went to Lydia's home; and when they had seen and encouraged the brothers and sisters there, they departed.

YOU PUSH THE STORY

What challenges and questions does this story pose for you? What is unbelievable? What would you ask the storyteller or the characters? What is intriguing? Look for background information related to these pushes in "The Story Behind the Story" on pages 128–130.

PUSH POSSIBILITIES FOR ACTS 16:13–40

- Why would Paul and Silas go to a river outside the city to find a place of prayer?

- This story reads like a film script with its vivid characters and explosive action. If you saw this as a movie, what would you understand about God and the early church when you left the theater?

- Is there anything unique about Lydia being baptized in the river?
- Why didn't Paul and Silas simply escape when the earthquake freed them?
- What's going on with the slave girl? What happens to her after the demon is cast out?
- What would salvation have meant to Lydia and the jailer?
- Why are Paul and Silas treated so harshly?
- Why are they in Philippi in the first place?

THE STORY PUSHES YOU

What new challenges does this story present to you? How is it comforting or healing? What unexpected or surprising word does it bring to you? What does it have to say to the church today?

- Lydia urges the apostles to come to her house. Have you experienced hospitality like that from people in churches? Have you extended it to others?
- Paul and Silas are beaten and sent to prison, but they do not get discouraged. What's the equivalent of their singing and praying late into the night for the way you live your faith?
- What does salvation mean to you?
- What do public acts of faith like baptism in the river, exorcism in the marketplace, imprisonment, and forcing a public apology suggest to us about our public witness?
- When have you witnessed the power of the gospel in conflict with the "powers that be"?
- This is a story of the early church—a church without walls, on the move, in the thick of things. What would you keep, change, or add to make today's church more like this one? What difference would it make in the world if you made those changes?

THE STORY BEHIND THE STORY

The biblical book of Acts is a collection of stories written by the same person who wrote the Gospel of Luke. The stories portray the ways that God's spirit expands the church beyond the original followers of Jesus, especially to Gentiles or non-Jews. These stories were meant to give Christians an unshakable confidence in the future of the church and the power of God's Spirit. In the stories, the apostles, meaning "those sent by God," travel to unfamiliar places north of the Mediterranean Sea to talk about Jesus Christ and set up churches in these areas. Eventually they establish a church in Philippi, as evidenced by the existence of a letter in the New Testament to the Philippians. All along their journeys these teachers and preachers endure hardships. They are arrested, they face shipwrecks, they are tortured, and some are even killed.

Philippi is a Roman colony, a center of government and commerce for its district. The Jewish community prayed outside the city walls by the river where they could have easy access to water for rituals of purification and libation. It is unclear whether there was an actual synagogue there. Among the Jewish women gathered by the river was Lydia, a seller of purple goods from Asia. We might imagine that Lydia was wealthy because purple cloth at the time was very expensive, being dyed with the rare coloring of the murex shellfish. Perhaps Lydia's baptism is related to a meeting of the apostles and the elders in Jerusalem (see the story in Acts 15) where they decided that it was legitimate to baptize those who were not circumcised (as a woman in this culture would not have been). Maybe she and her household were the first to test the newly expanded boundaries of community. Lydia's home becomes a base for the church in Philippi.

The next encounter in the story is of Paul ordering a spirit out of a slave girl who had been following the apostles around. It was quite common in the Greco-Roman world for the servants of powerful men to tell fortunes, earning lots of money for their masters. When Paul removes the spirit from this girl, her owners are out of a significant source of revenue. Angry, they create false charges against Paul and Silas, saying that these Jews with their customs of ritual purity and dietary restrictions were disrupting "their Roman way of life." Exorcism was not a legally punishable offense in the Roman Empire, but popular opinion was definitely against it. Paul and Silas were attacked by the crowds, beaten, and thrown in prison.

Sometimes stories like these are deliberately fantastic. Consider the earthquake in this story. It would have freed all of the prisoners, not just Paul and Silas. Presumably Paul and Silas are the only ones who stick around after it happens. They are focused on the jailer, who is about to kill himself because the other prisoners have escaped. We are not told whether this is a custom, or he is ashamed, or he fears punishment. What we do know from the story is that he is someone to be converted to the faith. As with Lydia, this represents an opening or expanding of the understanding of who can become part of the faith. The same council that allowed for the baptism of the uncircumcised stated that believers were to "abstain from what has been sacrificed to idols and from blood and from what is strangled"(Acts 15:20, 29). As a part of the Roman establishment, the prison guard would probably have eaten like a Roman, not according to Jewish dietary restrictions. He feeds Paul and Silas after cleaning their wounds. It seems the apostles are willing to stretch the boundaries of the church, eating like pagans, and baptizing an entire household of them to boot. It is ironic how far off base the charge of "advocating Jewish customs" is in terms of how Paul and Silas understood their mission.

Salvation is spoken of twice in the story, once by the slave-girl and once by the jailer. Salvation means wholeness and a right relationship with God. For the writer of Luke-Acts, the good news of Jesus Christ is that all people are invited to experience salvation.

When the authorities want to free the apostles quietly, Paul turns it into a public matter, demanding that the magistrates apologize for treating Roman citizens in such a manner. It is interesting that Paul waits until this moment, after all he and Silas go through, to reveal that they are Romans. Again the Spirit drives the disciples not just to seek their own security but also to publicly work for the building of the church, wherever they are. They refused to let the Christian faith be tarnished, and they refused to be victims of injustice.

PUSH OUT

You are invited to continue to "go public" with your faith through the following Push Out ideas.

- Take pictures of the people and places where you have encountered the holy. Consider the places where you have had great conversations, your favorite place in nature, places where you have offered service and were changed in the process by the people there, a meditation spot, a classroom where you have experienced growth, and persons who have pushed you in new ways. Create a Web site or find another way to share your journey with others.

- Increasingly, people in North America are able to expand their perspectives on the work of God in the world by engaging with people from faith communities different from their own. The Duncan Black Macdonald Center for the Study of Islam and Christian-Muslim Relations is a helpful resource that can be found at <www.macdonald.hartsem.edu>. How can you use resources from this center and others to develop projects that connect people of various faiths?

- Explore engagement in faith-based community organizing as a way to take a risk in the public arena. These organizations, established in cities all over North America, train leaders to be clear about their motivations for acting in community efforts. They encourage participants to become powerful people who work together to address the injustices of their community. The Gamaliel Foundation at <www.gamaliel.org/Foundation/foundation.htm>, Direct Action and Research Training (DART) at <dartcenter@aol.com>, and the Pacific Institute for Community Organizations (PICO) at <www.pico.rutgers.edu> are some of the national and international networks working with grassroots organizations.

- Share with others music you listen to that makes reference to a role in public life and discuss why it moves you.

- Find out how your faith tradition or denomination currently views the idea of "world mission" or global partnership with faith communities of other countries. As an example, go to the Web site <www.globalministries.org>. What do you notice about how the church's message is being reshaped by other cultures? How has the approach to people of faith in other countries changed over the years as our world has changed? How might these relationships change the way we in North American worship and serve? Explore more at the World Council of Churches Web site <www.wcc.org>. Are there ways you feel called to be involved?

GROUP IDEAS

[Focus: To explore the risks and possibilities of living faith "out loud" and in public.

LIFE'S A PUSH

■ Have the Bible story and push possibilities from page 124 available for participants. Have newsprint ready. Think about an experience you have had of being challenged for a faith position you have taken. Consider sharing that story as a way to get the group started.

■ Ask participants to read the two scenarios in "Life's a Push" on pages 124–125 and discuss responses to the questions provided.

■ Offer the prayer on page 125 or one of your own.

THE STORY

■ Read the story from Acts on pages 126–127 as a group. With so many characters and so much action, this story lends itself to the readers' theatre style. Have participants choose parts, including the narrator.

■ Select one or more ways to experience the story from suggestions on page 23. Select methods that allow participants to play with the details of the setting, such as painting or other arts media or movement.

YOU PUSH THE STORY

■ Invite participants to look over the possibilities listed on pages 127–128 and add their own on a piece of newsprint.

■ Have the group divide into two work teams and have each team focus on a story in the passage, one on the story of Lydia and one on the story of Paul and Silas being imprisoned. Have the teams explore the themes in their stories, using "The Story Behind the Story" on pages 128–130. Have the teams come back together to compare and contrast the two stories. What are the characters like? What's happening in the story? How do they push the stories?

■ Discuss the push possibilities on pages 127–128 and others the group suggests.

THE STORY PUSHES YOU

■ List on newsprint ways that the story challenges, judges, or heals.

■ Choose one of the pushes possibilities on page 128 and invite people to respond to it through journaling, sketching, or composing music.

PUSH OUT

- Select one or more of the "Push Out" experiences provided on pages 130–131. Plan a time to engage in the experience or experiences as a group.

- Offer the prayer below or one of your own.

PRAYER

Thank you, God, for your Spirit that moves us from secure places to places of risk. Help us to dare to live our faith out in the open, allowing our faith to empower us to act for justice and to connect with others. Amen.

13. [THE GREAT ORDEAL

And God will wipe every tear from their eyes.
Revelation 7:17

The visions in the book of Revelation are
mysterious and opaque, but a message of
comfort shines through.

IFE'S A PUSH

MY GREAT ORDEAL

At about 8:30 in the morning, I strode down the corridor to my wife Suzie's hospital room. I had brought her in the night before because she was weak from dehydration. Suzie had been taking codeine as a painkiller for an injury she sustained while practicing liturgical dancing at a conference for college students two days earlier. The codeine had stopped her digestive system; hospital tests indicated nothing other than severe constipation, a condition that a day or two in the hospital would easily address. I anticipated that she would still be sleeping when I got to her room.

Before I could get there, a doctor intercepted me, introduced himself, asked if I was "the husband," and then whisked me aside into an empty room, shut the door, and said, "As the nurse was checking on your wife a few moments ago, she couldn't find her pulse. I was nearby doing my morning rounds, so I was called in to administer cardio-pulmonary resuscitation. I was able to restore her heartbeat, though it is irregular, but she is still unconscious. Your wife is being transferred to the critical care unit (CCU), and you can go see her there in a few minutes."

He gave me directions to the CCU, and I was off down the hallway. Trying to remember the doctor's directions as I walked, my mind raced, my breathing started to escalate, and I found myself at a loss to know what to do next. Arriving in the CCU waiting room, I sat down in the first chair I could find, started welling up with tears, and began to recite the prayer Jesus taught his disciples (Matthew 6:9–15; Luke 11:1–4).

After what seemed like an eternity, a nurse came out, asked for me, and ushered me into the space where Suzie lay. Hooked up to numerous tubes, monitors, and machines, the only place I could find to touch her was on her forehead. As soon as I did, I could tell that Suzie was not there. Life, the spirit from God, had left her.

"It's okay, Suzie." I whispered. "Go. You're free now." To this day, I don't know where those words came from, but I knew they were true the moment I uttered them.

The specialists made their rounds throughout the day—all very informative, concerned, and kind, but none giving even a glint of hope for Suzie's recovery. They confirmed what I already knew. Later, I signed a "do not resuscitate" order, made some phone calls, and waited.

At dawn the next morning, about thirty-six hours after she was admitted to the hospital, Suzie's heart fluttered a few times and stopped again. My soul mate for over twenty-five years was dead. My great ordeal had begun.

YOUR GREAT ORDEAL

As human beings we all experience the downside of life on a regular basis. If we experience it in an especially intense way, we can consider ourselves to be having an "ordeal." If it's an ordeal at the edge of life and death, then it's a "great ordeal." For a community, a great ordeal is so serious that a much greater number of people die than survive while going through it. Perhaps you have already faced an ordeal in your life; perhaps not. Whatever your personal experience has been, human history is filled with many great ordeals.

- Have you had or are you presently having a "great ordeal" in your life? What brings you comfort and solace?

- If you haven't had a great ordeal in your life, where or among whom can you identify a great ordeal that has occurred or is presently occurring?

- What do you think could have transformed or would be needed to transform the great ordeal situation?

PRAYER

O Great One, we praise you for the life you have given to all living beings. We recognize also that life involves suffering, sometimes great suffering. May you teach us patience and discernment so that when the times of trial come we will be able to endure them and to know what to do. Amen.

THE STORY

Read the text from Revelation 7:9–17. If you want, select a way to experience the story from the suggestions listed on page 23.

⁹After this I looked, and there was a great multitude that no one could count, from every nation, from all tribes and peoples and languages, standing before the throne and before the Lamb, robed in white, with palm branches in their hands. ¹⁰They cried out in a loud voice, saying,

> "Salvation belongs to our God
> who is seated on the
> throne, and to the Lamb!"

¹¹And all the angels stood around the throne and around the elders and the four living creatures, and they fell on their faces before the throne and worshiped God, ¹²singing,

> "Amen! Blessing and glory
> and wisdom
> and thanksgiving and honor
> and power and might
> be to our God forever and ever!
> Amen."

¹³Then one of the elders addressed me, saying, "Who are these, robed in white, and where have they come from?" ¹⁴I said to him, "Sir, you are the one that knows." Then he said to me, "These are they who have come out of the great ordeal; they have washed their robes and made them white in the blood of the Lamb.

> ¹⁵For this reason they are before the
> throne of God,
> and worship him day and night
> within the temple,
> and the one who is seated on
> the throne will shelter
> them,

> ¹⁶They will hunger no more, and
> thirst no more;
> the sun will not strike them,
> nor any scorching heat;
> ¹⁷for the Lamb at the center of the
> throne will be their
> shepherd,
> and he will guide them to
> springs of the water of life,
> and God will wipe away every
> tear from their eyes."

YOU PUSH THE STORY

This text is in the center of a mind-boggling prophetic narrative, so there is a lot to push against. What do you find most outrageous about the imagery described? Does anything offend you? Make you feel queasy? Can you identify any comfortable images? Push with your impressions, your questions, and your comments in addition to the suggestions below. Then seek possible ways to begin addressing some of those questions in the section entitled "The Story Behind the Story" on pages 138–140.

PUSH POSSIBILITIES FOR REVELATION 7:9–17

- Who is the "I" and what is the "this" in, "After this I looked . . . " in verse 9?
- Why couldn't the multitude be counted? Who makes up the multitude, and what are they doing there?
- Why is "Lamb" in verse 10 capitalized? To whom or what does it refer?
- Who are the elders and what do they signify? The four living creatures?
- What is the "great ordeal" in verse 14?
- To what does the "blood of the Lamb" refer?
- How does the great multitude manage to worship "24/7" without getting hungry or thirsty or burned from the bright light?
- How can God wipe away tears?

THE STORY PUSHES YOU

Now allow the story to push you in return. What images might stretch your assumptions about the world and God's activity in it? Are there images that introduce you to realities you have never thought of? If so, what are they?

PUSH POSSIBILITIES FOR REVELATION 7:9–17

- If you can visualize yourself as one of the great multitude, what do you think that experience would feel like?

- What do you think you would have to do to "wash your robe" to "make it white" (v. 14)? Why would you? Why would your robe need cleaning?

- What powers does the prophet's vision ascribe to the Lamb in this passage? What importance do these powers have to you?

- Why do you think worship is so important in this visionary scene, especially for the great multitude? How central is worship to you and why?

- How can verses 15–17 be understood as comforting? Why are the images so "earthy"?

- Have you ever been comforted by God "wiping away" your tears? If so, how did that happen?

THE STORY BEHIND THE STORY

The Revelation to John is probably the most misunderstood book in the Christian Bible. It is easily misunderstood because it was *intentionally* written to be difficult to understand, one of the underlying purposes of apocalyptic literature generally. This genre—from the Greek word *apocalypses* ("unveiling" or "disclosing")—developed among persecuted Jewish communities in the second century BC and was adapted for Christian purposes through the second century CE. Its use of cryptic symbolism and nonlinear structure kept it from being readily understood by the mainstream powers that oppressed these communities. Apocalyptic literature employs a sophisticated code language that relies on an intimate knowledge of the Hebrew Scriptures and creative use of word-images to communicate its message. It heralds the final fulfillment of God's purposes for creation and God's vindication against evil. The apocalyptic perspective is often misunderstood to be "other-worldly," yet this angle is one of the only avenues available to communities with absolutely no access to power in this world. The other world becomes the source of that power in *this* world.

The cultural and political context of the Revelation is marked by the intensification of emperor worship during the reign of Domitian (81–96 CE). Though Roman emperors were long considered divine, their role in Roman civil religion was not enforced until late in the first century. Then, citizens across the empire were required to appear annually before a magistrate to burn a pinch of incense and declare, "Caesar is Sovereign." Though this practice was probably understood more as fulfilling a civic duty than making a statement of faith, for Christians to declare anyone else as sovereign conflicted with their understanding that "Jesus is Sovereign." So Roman authorities persecuted the Christians to the point of death. This is the situation that the Revelation addresses by portraying the final victory of the Sovereign Christ over the beastly power of Rome claiming sovereignty that only the living God can grant. Such a message fueled hope among beleaguered Christian communities on the edge of despair, even as they endured the great ordeal of persecution and martyrdom by the hands of Rome.

Though considering the original context is essential to decoding its symbols and understanding its message, the book speaks beyond its own time to address realities such as good versus evil, faith versus apostasy, and the consummation of all things by God's plan. This is why the book was included in the Christian canon and why it still contains power and insights for Christians today.

The book is organized according to a series of five septenaries, or groups of seven. Chapters 1–3 report letters to seven churches in Asia Minor representing the historic church in time, "the already" promise. Chapters 5–7 describe the seven seals, the backbone of the book, which disclose the domain of God's power on earth. Chapters 8–14 detail the seven trumpets that set in motion the disclosures given previously. God unites with creation to wage war against evil, to die, and then become victorious. Chapter 16 portrays the seven bowls of wrath, God's ultimate vindication against evil. Chapters 19–22 reveal "The New Creation" or the church beyond time in the "not yet" fulfillment by using the device, "Then I saw," seven times to highlight each point. The chapters that don't fit this septenary structure underscore the importance of worshiping the living God, one of the central themes of the book. Chapters 4 and 15 describe true worship of God, while chapters 17–18 portray false worship and the destruction of the Great Whore and the fall of Babylon (i.e., the false objects of worship, Rome and its emperors). Worship of the true God was the reason for and consolation during the persecution these Christian communities endured. It was also the source of their power to resist Roman oppression.

The seventh chapter of the Revelation describes two visions and functions as an interlude between the opening of the sixth and seventh seal. The burden of the visions is to assure the faithful that they are held safely in God's embrace, that is, "sealed" from what is about to be disclosed. The "countable" group is the 144,000 sealed out of Israel's twelve tribes that are then listed in 7:5–8. As with almost everything in the Revelation, the 144,000 is not to be taken literally; rather it is the full perfection of Israel's faith or possibly Jewish Christians represented by the result of 12 times 12. The contrast of this rendering with what follows in verse 7:9 is striking. Here the prophet sees "a great multitude *that no one could count*, from every nation, from all tribes and peoples and languages" (author's emphasis). This multitude is nothing less than the universal church in and beyond time—the meaning of a "countless" multitude.

To understand better the beings mentioned around God's throne in 7:11, see chapter 4, where the royal scene is described in much more detail. The writer of the Revelation was clearly inspired by similar images found in earlier prophets such as Daniel, Isaiah, Ezekiel, and Zechariah. The prophet used the imagery of his time to convey powerful forces that were active in his community's experience. The twenty-four elders represent the faithful leaders of the church, rooted as it was in Judaism. The four living creatures represent the four corners of the earth, that is, all of creation. The Lamb and its role in 7:10, 14, and 17 is described more fully in 5:1–8. The association of the Lamb with Christ is unmistakable, yet the creativity employed in the imagery is amazing. (For an artist's rendering of such imagery, try to find an image of painter Jan van Eyck's *Adoration of the Mystic Lamb*, part of the Ghent Altarpiece in Vijd Chapel, Cathedral St. Bravo, Ghent, Belgium.) The power of Christ's suffering and death, symbolized by blood, is sufficient to grant righteousness and purity to the great multitude, symbolized by white robes (7:14), and ultimate victory, symbolized by palm branches (7:9). The blood symbol is especially powerful since it interprets the meaning of the actual martyrdom that the Roman Christians experienced, identifying their martyrdom directly with Christ's.

PUSH OUT

This text directs attention to the down side of faith as a great ordeal and the up side of faith as God's promise to comfort and protect the faithful. The following are some suggestions about how you might explore these dynamics of faith and the interplay between them.

- Find someone who has experienced a major loss relatively recently (the death of a loved one, unemployment, serious illness), and ask them if you can interview them about how they experienced their loss and how their faith did or did not help them cope with the loss.

- Learn about the Christian church in a part of the world where it is not in the majority such as in Indonesia, North Africa, the Middle East, India, China, or Japan, paying particular attention to how the church understands itself in relation to the culture in which it lives, especially the continuities and discontinuities, and what role the gospel plays in these relationships. Perhaps a Christian from that part of the world lives in your community, and they might tell you about what church life is like back home.

- Living in a post-September 11 time, major military conflict is more likely than it has been in many years. If such a conflagration occurs, Christians, particularly in the United States, may need to make decisions about serving in the armed forces. What would you do? How would you define "patriotism" in such a situation? What role does your faith play in facing these decisions?

- Some Christians feel that their faith in Jesus Christ, the Prince of Peace, means that they must oppose warfare and violence as a means to settle disputes. If you want to explore this option or discover whether you might be a "conscientious objector" according to U.S. federal law, visit the Web site of the National Interreligious Board for Conscientious Objectors at <www.nisb-co.org>.

  Information about conscientious objection in Canada, including conscientious objectors' registry resources, is available from the Mennonite Church Web site at <www.mennonitechurch.ca/resources/sept11/sept11cobjection.html>.

- View the video *Sophie's Choice* (ITC Films, Inc., CBS/Fox Video; dir. Alan Pakula, 1982) and reflect on the role of hope among persecuted Jews going through a great ordeal under Hitler's Third Reich. Alternatively, view the movie *Romero* (Vidmark Entertainment; dir. John Duigan, 1997) for a glimpse into the great ordeal of those living in abject poverty in Central America and the response of one seminal church leader. How is Romero's work like the vision of Revelation?

- Imagine a situation when the government would challenge or perhaps even close your church for its lack of compliance with the laws of the land. What might bring that on? How do you think your church would respond? How would you respond?

- Alone or with a group, visit an art museum and look for examples of apocalyptic art. How is this imagery similar to and different from images in the book of Revelation?

- Ask the choir director or minister of music of your church to locate a choral setting of "God Shall Wipe Away All Tears." Sing it with a group during worship.

GROUP IDEAS

[Focus: To engage the prophetic imagery of Revelation in ways that shape our faith and bring us words of hope and comfort in the midst of great ordeals.

LIFE'S A PUSH

- Read and then discuss "My Great Ordeal" on pages 134–135. What makes the circumstances a great ordeal for the author?

- Read the first paragraph under "Your Great Ordeal" on page 135 and discuss examples of a great ordeal both in history and in participants' lives. Discuss the questions on page 135.

- As the discussion winds down, pray the prayer provided on page 135 or one of your own. You could also chant the words of Revelation 7:9b: "Salvation belongs to our God who is seated on the throne, and to the Lamb."

THE STORY

- Before encountering the text on pages 136–137 for the first time as a group, prepare participants by giving them these instructions: "Imagine that your government demands unqualified allegiance to its leader, the government, and its policies. If you fail to comply, you will be arrested, perhaps tortured, or even executed. As a Christian, you find that you cannot comply. How would you describe or illustrate your resistance? Use paint, markers, and crayons to draw, if you like, or write a description that outlines the issues, strategies, and final outcomes of the struggle to maintain your faith." Ask them to save their work for discussion later.

- To engage the text, first assign one or more participants to each of these roles:

  a great multitude
  the throne
  the Lamb
  the angels
  the elders or one of the elders
  the four living creatures
  the prophet (the "I" in the narrative)
  a reader

  Then, as the reader reads the text very slowly, each role player responds with a gesture or simple movement to what the reader reads. Try to arrange the role players at the beginning so that their actions can be carried out in a way that corresponds to the reading (e.g., the prophet needs to be some distance from the court scene so that she or he can "look" at it [v. 7:9]).

■ As an alternative to the acting method above, role players could read lines as in a script-reading for a play. Not all the roles have lines, so perhaps a mix of reciting and simple movements can be done.

■ For other possibilities to engage the text, see the suggestions on page 23.

YOU PUSH THE STORY

■ Ask participants to present and discuss the art they created for the item above in "The Story."

■ Brainstorm questions about the text. Include those from the listed of push possibilities on page 137 that are of interest to participants.

■ Either as a group or in pairs, ask participants to try answering these questions by referring to "The Story Behind the Story" on page 138–140. Have participants note which ones they couldn't answer and have them propose a method that they might use to find out the answers.

THE STORY PUSHES YOU

■ Ask participants how the text might challenge them to think differently about the Christian faith, the church, or themselves.

■ Use the list of push possibilities on page 138 to continue the discussion.

PUSH OUT

■ Ask participants to choose one suggestion on pages 141–142 that they will either do on their own or as a group. If the latter, have them schedule a time to do it.

■ If there is interest among participants, schedule a follow-up session after a reasonable time has passed for everyone to do one of the push out activities on pages 141–142. Participants can share what they learned and how the activity affected them.

■ Offer the prayer below or pray one of your own to conclude the session.

PRAYER

O visionary God, who comes to us in extravagant and extraordinary images, grant that we may learn better to see you in new and different places, among new and different peoples, that we might more closely follow the path of your purposes for us on this earth. Amen.

CONTRIBUTORS

]

Several contributors to *Push It!* Volume 4 work with Local Church Ministries, a Covenanted Ministry of the United Church of Christ in Cleveland, Ohio:

JANA NORMAN, editor, is the Minister for Curriculum Development.

SIDNEY D. FOWLER wrote the introduction, "What's the Push All About?" He is the Minister for Worship, Liturgy, and Spiritual Formation.

GLORIA OTIS, Administrative Staff for Worship and Education, wrote the article "On Staying Open to the Spirit: An Article for Push It! Group Leaders on Creating a Quality Learning Community" and session 9.

BRUCE LARSON is the Minister for Campus and Student Ministries. He wrote session 13.

TERRY YASUKO OGAWA, the Charles E. Cobb Environmental Justice Resident at the Public Life and Social Policy Ministry of the United Church of Christ in Washington, D.C., wrote sessions 1 and 2.

HELEN R. NEINAST is a former United Methodist campus minister at Emory University in Atlanta who now lives in north Georgia where she writes and lead retreats with her husband Tom Ettinger. Helen wrote sessions 3, 5, and 6.

MONA BAGASAO CAVE wrote sessions 4, 10, and 11. She is the Director of Campus Ministries and the Chaplain at Eckerd College in St. Petersburg, Florida.

CRAIG SCHAUB, wrote sessions 7, 8, and 12. He also wrote the article, "Ideas for Deepening the Connection to the Bible." Craig is co–pastor of Plymouth Congregational United Church of Christ in Syracuse, New York.